TELL'EM ANYTHING

(Facing the Corporate Idiot!)

TELL'EM ANYTHING

(Facing the Corporate Idiot!)

BY

RUSSELL MAYES

This book was inspired by true stories associated with Russell Mayes. Names were changed for the protection of others involved. Situation that resembles people or companies are purely coincidental and unintended and should not be taken as fact.

Copyright © 2000 by Russell Mayes
All rights reserved.
No part of this book may be reproduced, stored in a retrieval system, or transmitted by any means, electronic, mechanical, photocopying, recording, or otherwise, without written permission from the author.

ISBN: 1-58721-755-4

1stBooks – rev. 5/25/00

About the Book

"TELL'EM ANYTHING " is an inside look at the way corporation see and view their employees and corporate rules and regulations as seen through the eyes of Russell Mayes.

Both entertaining and true to life situations "TELL'EM ANYTHING" (facing the corporate idiot) will make you think and laugh at the way the corporate world sees itself while look down through the glass floor.

ACKNOWLEDGMENT

I would like to thank the people that helped in preparing this book; my brother John and Terri Mayes, my good friends Kathy Greenaway, and James Patterson.

This book was written with hopes that others would see the light of handing over their lives to a corporation in hopes of that that company would take care of them and their families. That hope is nothing but a dream blinder supplied by the corporations to keep employees from questioning authority.You must envision your own future; you must strive to achieve your own destiny. If that destiny is to climb the corporate ladder then do it with full dedication. If you see your future in other areas or the company does not care for your views and just wants a robot then move on. These are all judgment calls and you must follow your own path.

"Dreams and Ideas are the seeds for the future"

TABLE OF CONTENTS

ACKNOWLEDGMENT vii

SO YOU'RE LATE 1

INTERNAL DEALINGS 13

CYA COVER YOUR ASS 35

IN THE MEN'S ROOM 55

LUNCH 61

PAYDAY 67

SUPPLY AND DEMAND 71

THE GET AWAY 77

WORK PALS 83

SIGNS OF THE TIMES 103

TIME OFF 119

FORWARD

In our society we are taught about work ethics and how we should act in the face of the corporate hierarchy. This is the teaching that has been handed down through the decades and is reinforced by the school system. We are molded into the fabric of our society from birth. We are taught to depend on the system, that the system will be there when we need it.

This is one of the biggest lies that have been perpetrated on the public for as long as man has had organizations. This however is a necessary evil. The reason that I say it is necessary is because we as human beings cannot survive on this planet without organizations.

So we have two choices in which to live our lives. Let someone else decide how that life is to be lived or live that life yourself.

It seems pretty simple and a basic enough concept. But the more and more people that become reliant on the system the more and more powerful the system becomes.

Let me say one thing, there are always exceptions to the rule. No matter how good or thorough they are something always happens to upset what has been put into place, this is known to many as "MURPHY'S LAW".

For instance, let us look at the Kennedy assassination. I am not here to say one or many did it. However if it were not for the "ZAPRUDER" film, we would not have had all the controversy. It would have gone down in history as a single shooter, end of story. But unforeseen things happen in the best of plans. I have been involved in many propaganda promotions from the Military to the Corporate Giants. These propaganda promotions range from the serious to morale building. They are played out in slow or fast, depending on the goal of the campaign. Information in our world is the most important factor in our lives. We need to know when the trains and planes are running. We need to know what time to be at work, we need to know when to eat, sleep, and even make time to go to the restroom. Kick back and think about how your life is structured so that you can fit into a functioning society. We need this functioning society to live our lives; we depend on each other to make it from day to day. We take the dream to heart and we work ourselves to death to achieve the dreams that have been placed in front of us. The dream is as follows a spouse, a house, a car, 2.5 kids, a cat, a dog, and the fairy godmother to make it all work. In school this is what was taught to us as the American Dream. But they never told us how to get it. So we graduate and end up working in a Job and hoping that we win the lottery, so the "Man" can take half in taxes, and pay us the rest in payments, without interest of course, because the man feels we are not able to handle large sums of money. Which is true because they never taught us how in their school system. I must tell you now that this book in not about bringing down the government or creating riots or even saving the whales. It is however stories about how to deal with idiocies within the corporate work place. We all know about how management and the corporate structure are not about making it a better place to work. Even though that is what they tell us. It is about what to tell your superiors when they confront you with an idiotic suggestion that they want you to carry out, in which they will never check to see if you have done what they asked. The reason is because they were told by there higher ups to tell you. And the higher ups do not check them either. Everyone is here to keep his or her job and nothing more. If someone comes up to you and tells you that they are not that way, ask them to do it for free! In the following pages are stories and suggestions on what to do when you are confronted with the stupid and how to deal with it so you can keep your job until a better one comes a long. I am telling you straight, if you think your position is secure you are fooling yourself and everyone around you. I have been there and have made those decisions, and the easiest decision for any company to save money is to cut back on its work force. I know there will be people that tell me that I am full of it. Well my answer to that is, prove me wrong! Job Security is where corporation tell their employees that they are secure at their jobs. Then, the next day they find the doors to the factory closed and their retirement fund gone.

In the pages that follow, you will find situations that I have come up against and some solutions as to what I did to either avoid or solve those confrontations with the corporate idiots.

SO YOU'RE LATE

Being late is one of the most violated rules for any company. It carries with it the highest reasons for excuses.

In the summer of 82, I was fresh out of the military and was working at a local factory. I was hired on for the midnight shift, which was and still is in my opinion the worst shift anyone can hold. Your whole life is screwed; you watch soap operas because there is nothing else on the tube at that time in the day. All your friends are at work, and the only people that are around are the people that you work with. Well the system was in place, my life had gone down the tubes real fast and I jumped on the Drug and booze bandwagon as fast as I could. It was the only way to kill the pain of the job. The company continued to tell us that working this shift was the best and because of that we were paid an extra 25 cents and hour for doing our part. Can you believe that! 25 cents so the man can make his millions. But I bought into the concept that I was doing it for the company. As the year wore on the amount of time that I came in late started to increase. So every time that I was late, my foreman would run up to me as I was punching in on the time clock. He would start the typical corporate run of the mill questions and statements straight out of the corporate manual. It must have had every answer that has ever been told to a foreman in past history. He was good at coming up with reasons why my excuses were not any good for him to allow me to be late.

I guess it was the system I was afraid of; I was scared to say anything that would set him off. I did not want to loose my security or the paycheck that I bought all my booze and drugs with just so I can continue to work at a place as mind numbing as factory work.

Day in and day out I gave my soul to that place to make bearings as fast as I could, just so I could receive that paycheck to buy my life which was going down the tubes fast. It was piecework, that any factor production worker can tell you, is good and bad. It all depends on how you look at it. Just imagine clocking in and walking up to a cast iron dust covered machine. There are six stations to the one work place. The cycle goes in a circle and it takes 56 seconds to run one bearing. Now do this for 8 to 10 hours a day. You talk about mind numbing and robotic work. I do not want to put anyone down, but if you started out that way like many of the old timers did, they did not know there was a life outside the walls of industry. Which is why corporations do not like free thinkers in the first place. They would not have a work force if the workers knew they could make the same amount of money using their heads. Instead, they let the company use their bodies. The company told many stories about how great we were doing and they even gave awards to the highest producer of product. Sometimes they even gave a day off for good work with pay! I can tell you the bullshit piled up fast in that place. So anyway I came running in one day after the many days that I was late. And he was standing there with his book in hand and ready for gunfire. He came up to me and yelled "WHY ARE YOU LATE"! I stopped in my tracks and looked him straight in the eye, and said "THE SKY IS BLUE"! With that I turned and headed for my machine. I noticed that everyone within earshot was looking at me with shock on their faces. I was even thinking to myself that I was cooked. I had broken a rule of management engagement. You shall not make waves to the manager. This was written in the stone of the corporate gods whom controlled my life and everything in it. I knew a bolt of lightning was headed my way. As I dove into the locker room to put on my work boots and clothing to protect myself from the onslaught of hot metal chips that pelted me from the lathe. I glanced back and saw a sight I was not expecting. He was still standing there watching me. He had a blank stare on his face. It was like he had not processed the information at hand. He looked like his computer locked up and needed rebooting.

So I took the time to jump into my clothes and hit my machine as fast as I could. It took more than 2 hours before he came up to me to ask what the hell I was talking about!

There I was running in the circle that the company said I had to do. This all-powerful man came up to me and waited until the lathe and the machine finished their cycles. He reached up and slammed the emergency switch and all my machines came to a screeching halt. I turned and the fear of the corporation filled me, I knew I was done. My mind was racing and all I could think of was get my toolbox and leave. Then it happened, he spoke. What he said next, to this day I could not believe. He looked me straight in the eyes and said, "WHAT THE HELL DID YOU MEAN BY THAT"? At that moment I knew I was a better man than this thing that controlled my life. I knew that even if I got fired that I was better than this dehumanizing place of work. I also knew if I did not get fired I would still be better than this place of work. I thought for many days and weeks even, about that one moment in time. I knew I did not have to do what they wanted unless I wanted to do it. They did not control me. They did not care about me. They did not even want to know if I was human. All they wanted was someone to run the machines and produce the products. I was a machine to them, and now the machine had questioned their existence and they did not know how to deal with it. The reason that this poor man did not know how to deal with me, is because the corporation did not tell him how to handle a situation like that. Yes there are managers and foreman that know how and would have dealt with the situation differently. But you must realize even the managers that knew the proper response to the situation, were taught by the corporation that they worked for.

So as my confidence grew inside me, I knew that I was no longer a machine, I was a human being. I still might have been a newborn but I was human finally. I was a decision maker, in control of my own life. I felt like superman coming out of the phone booth for the first time. I was MAN! All I needed was the music from 2001 A SPACE ODYSSEY and the moment would have been complete. I looked him in the eye and told him straight out. "YOU NEEDED AN EXCUSE SO I GAVE YOU ONE". For a moment it became a staring contest. He did not know what to do. So he said "IS THAT ALL YOUR GOING TO TELL ME?" my answer was "YES" he looked at me and said "FINE". The rest of the night went along ok, however all my co-workers were watching every move I made. They were also watching every move the Foreman made. I could not believe that these workers gave their lives to this company who treated them like dirt, and they thanked the company for the dirt they got.

My god the gossip ran through that building like a wild fire on a hot afternoon. They were all waiting for the bomb to be dropped on me and they all wanted to see it. I had worked with these guys for a few years and I was their entertainment for the night. It was something new and it was exciting to them. I could not believe it. A small altercation such as this made the dull and dreary place come alive. It seemed like everyone was walking with a spring in their step and their machines worked better, and they even enjoyed their lunch. However when I walked into the lunchroom you could hear a pin drop in there. Now this made me a little uncomfortable, because these were people that I thought were apart of me and would stand beside me when the chips are down. Well another rude awakening hit me in the face. They were scared that some of the vibes would rub off and get them fired too. So during the shift it was like I had the plague or leprosy. I was in shock; I did not realize that the power of corporate control was so ingrained into these people. I knew then no matter what came out of the incident, my time at this company was numbered. Whether they found a way to make me leave or if I left myself, I was no longer a member of this corporate family, as they would like you to think.

What was good, was my mind started to think like a man again who was in control of his future. I did not know what I wanted to do with my life; all I knew was that I could do anything I wanted. How many of you have really thought about that? You can do what ever you want! The problem is that school never taught me to think like this. I was scared and nervous. What was I going to do? How would I live without the income that the corporate mother gave me to eat? How could I pay the rent, it is amazing how the mind can rationalize the degradation that a corporation can place on you and make it feel like it is good.

This fear that companies use to control their employees, is very important to the everyday operations of many companies. Think about when you were a teenager and wanting to get your first job. You were scared and wanted to make a good impression. But at the same time you wanted to express your own sense of freedom and prove to the world that you are not controlled by the system. Being a teenager and working at a theme park with roller coasters and wild and exciting rides has got to be a dream come true to the everyday young adult. However even working at a place as exciting as that carries the corporate structure of rules and regulations, just like any company you work for. So being carefree and wild at heart, you try to beat the system. But beating the system at a young age means that you are not experienced enough to understand the powers that are against you. You even think you can out wit the system for those few moments of fun. For example, one summer day in Southern California, My coworkers and I had been working for a theme park as ride operators and vendors and doing various jobs within the park. It was the thing to do if you were a kid in Southern California. Everyone worked at the park at least once in their life before they knew what they wanted to do. It is like fast food in other areas of the country. However you even get fast food in the park. Now if that doesn't suck. To work for a fast food company in a theme park, anyway we were always trying to beat the system. But the system had us in its grip and we didn't even know it. The managers were only a few years older than we and they were taught that they had the power over the younger employees. So you had a bunch of twenty year olds running around thinking that they were masters over you. So in retaliation we would try to do anything that would prove that we were better than they were. This one summer day we were cruising to work and listening to the radio. The four of us, you know the buddy thing. The same guys that you went to high school and partied with every weekend. Partying until you passed out and hoped that your buds would be kind enough not to mess with you and make sure that you got to a safe place to sleep it off.

Well anyway, we were on the freeway heading to work when on the radio they announced that Journey was playing in concert. "Oh man can you believe it"! I said. Everyone in the car agreed it was a real deal and we had to go. At any price we were going to rock the day away. So we knew we had to go, so we stopped the car at a convenient store along the way. I grabbed a few dimes; yes phone calls were a dime at that time. So I called the supervisor in charge of my area. I told him that the engine in my car blew up and since I was the man with the wheels, and since all my friends rode with me, none of us would be in to work today.

It was fool proof; we would be off to the concert as soon as we got our paychecks cashed. So we pulled in to the payroll office and picked up the checks and we were off. Now since none of us had checking accounts or any other way of cashing the checks that we had in our hands. We soon realized that we had to go to the bank, which happened to be on park grounds. So here is the problem, I told the boss that the motor was gone. If we got caught cashing our checks at the park bank, the question would be how did you get there if your car was trashed? This ordeal turned into an adventure in itself. We knew that the bank was at the front of the park. We also knew that we could get in through the front gates with our badges. However the supervisor's office was next to the bank. Now I ask you, do you think that they put that office there for a reason? We had to make a battle plan. Each person had to cash their own check, so we could not all go in at the same time. So the plan was I would go first to see if the coast was clear, then the others would follow in intervals of one minute. That way we could all meet in the bank and not look like we came together.

So the plan was set, I took off thinking of anything to say to the man if he saw me. Excuses ran through my head. My mom brought me in; she is waiting in the car. Or my dad brought me in; he is waiting in the car. Or my sister drove me here to pick up my check; she is waiting in the car. I mumbled these thoughts in my head as I came closer and closer to the office. I was scared shitless inside; my stomach was turning inside and out. I knew that if I got caught, it would be the gas chamber for sure. I heard stories from the bosses of what they did to employees that skipped out on work. They told that if we were caught doing things of this nature that I would never be able to work again. That they would ruin my life and any chances to graduate from high school or even get into a college. I would end up digging ditches in some god-forsaken country. The sweat was pouring from my brow. I looked into the window of the office as I passed by. No one was in; I began to relax once I knew that he was not there. I turned the corner and entered the bank. It had a few people in it, all were standing in line to cash their checks. I took my check out and signed the back of it at a table in the corner. I then took my place in line. As I stood there, in walked the rest of the gang, they were trying to act as if it was a coincident that we all happened to be at the bank at the same time. Now we were trapped like rats, standing in line and those dam line ropes held us at bay. We had to move with the line. It is what we were taught, to step over those ropes meant certain death or a mean stare from a customer or teller. My turn finally came; I cashed my check and got the money. I knew at that moment how Jesse James felt robbing the banks of his days. My friends watched me as I passed the door to freedom. A smile came over me as I opened the door. I knew Journey was just around the corner and it was good times ahead! What happened next is considered funny now, but at the time it was the worst experience I have ever encountered. Standing in the door was the man! He was on his way in to cash his check. We stood at high noon the sun was blaring down the town clock was ticking the seconds away. What was I going to do? I knew that death had come and my life was ruined. I had to say something and say it fast. Time seemed to slow down to the point of stopping. My friends seem to blow by us without ever stopping. I looked around I saw mothers taking their children off the street and out of harms way. I looked at my money in my hand and then looked him in the eye and said. "MY GRANDMOTHER IS UNDER THE CAR"! I bolted out the door and did not turn back to see if he was chasing me, or what he was going to do.

Now comes the hindsight, the man knew that I had a brand new car. Also even if he did not confront me at the bank, how did I get my check and cash it? Plus from the time I called him to the time of bank cashing. It was way to close, it was a 40-minute drive to the park and it took us 15 minutes to get and cash our checks. Also by the time we got to the concert, it was sold out and we ended up eating at a fast food joint and wasting the day away.

I could not believe how much fear I carried with me about losing a job of minimum wage. How much control of my life I allowed the system to have over me.

We see this in everything we do from work to play. We have been programmed to conduct ourselves in a way that is acceptable to what we think society is and what it should be. This way of thinking filters down from your place of work and it permeates your personal life and that of your children. Without you even knowing about it. You make decisions at home that have a direct effect on your work schedule. Case in point; one of the most interesting excuses ever used on me was one that did not come from the mind of the teenager who was in possession of it.

It was a normal day and the restaurant was moderately busy. We had a steady flow of customers all morning. One of my employees we'll call her, "Sue" just for the heck of it, had called in and left a message with one of her friends who happened to be the very one that Sue covered for last week. I was handed the note stating, "SUE COULD NOT WORK TODAY BECAUSE SHE HAS TO WAIT FOR THE CABLE GUY"! I looked at the note and read it and then I read it again. I could not help it, a smile broke across my face. I could not believe what I was reading! I folded the note up and stuck it in my pocket and headed back into the kitchen. I confronted "Betty" (not her real name either). OK fine I changed the names to protect the innocent. And if you think any of these kids are innocent you are living in a dream world. I hate to be the one to break it to the world, but this generation of kids or teens are very smart and since they were raised more on a latch key situation they are even street wise. But the only thing a company or parent have going for them is experience. The teens know that not much can be done to them in the way of punishment. Because we have taken the control of discipline out of the hands of the family and put it in the hands of the system and the system does not care about the kids one way or the other. As I walked up to Betty, who saw me coming and knew what I wanted before I even said a word. Out of her mouth came, "I WAS RELAYING A MESSAGE AND THAT IS ALL!" "take it easy Betty" I am not going to kill you because of what your friends do. That would be way to easy. I love busting them when they do stupid things. However I never humiliate them in front of their friends. That is one sure way to lose two or three employees at once. Teens never do anything alone. They must have and audience or others to back them up. So if one walks they all walk, I have seen it many times before. But if the others do not know why their friend was canned, they do not have the guts to walk or make up their own minds by themselves.

I pulled the note out and pointed to it, and asked "IS THIS FOR REAL?" the answer that I got next is without a doubt a classic in the world of the teens. "DAHH" I tell you that one cracks me up every time I hear it. It is the answer for every thing. Do you think he's cute? DAHH, did you think that was a good movie? DAHH! Do you think your going to be fired!? DAHH, I did use that once. It was great. So since she had told me just what I wanted to hear. I turned and headed to the office to confirm the information at hand. I pulled her file out and called her house. Sue did answer the phone, which shocked me. I said Sue this is work what is this I hear about you having to wait for the Cable Guy? It was true, her dad told her that she had to wait at home and not go to work because he and her mother had to work and in their minds their jobs were more important than that of their daughters. I knew that she was in hell. She could not hit the town, which she would have done if she was making up excuses. So in my infinite wisdom I decided to call her every hour or so, because she had to answer the phone, just in case it was the cable guy. Of course all her loyal friends were behind me one hundred percent.

It is really amazing to hear and think up some of the reasons for not coming in on time. The really scary part to all this is, a lot of it makes sense at the time of conception of the idea. Afterwards you think to yourself, "DID THEY REALLY BUY THAT LAME ASS EXCUSE"? The true answer is NO; they just needed an excuse to tell their higher ups. They, as in the management and bosses over you could not care less if you were late or early. Unless they had to fill in for you, then they would be extremely pissed. If the position could operate without you there for a day, "so be it", would be their thoughts for the day. I swear I use to work with a guy that his car would always break down. This mini van that he drove must have been a rattrap, however it was fine on weekends and times he needed to do personal shit. But the best or most original reason for being late was this one-day. We started shifts early, so dammed early that the sun was not up yet. I hate getting up early and going to a job that gives you no satisfaction, with all your superiors so on edge as to weather they have a job each day did nothing but put me on edge. Now that to me is no way to run a corporation. I have never seen so many stressed out people in one place in my entire life. Check this out, working on a movie set, now that is stress, millions of dollars riding on every minute that film is not finished. You start at 5 in the morning, which means you are up at 3. You shoot all day and get off around 11 at night sometimes later. This lasts for a few months then you rest. But the great part is, everyone that is on the set wants to be there. They mumble a little and have the coffee and doughnuts and they are off and at it. Everyone on the set loves the job. It is hard work, good pay, and good people. Everyone is neurotic and needs psychiatric care but what a gang of people.

Anyway let me get back to what we all think is a real job. And the reason we think it is a real job is because we are afraid to go out and stake a claim in life. We need big brother watching over us. We want to make sure we are safe and comfy in our worlds. Until big brother decides to make a change in the work force because he or she cannot make the yacht payments this month.

So one day I'll call him Bill, So Bill calls in and tells the boss man that he is going to be late not because he over slept, oh no, that is a no no. Even though it is the truth, but we cannot tell the truth or you will be punished. You must lie and pretend it is the truth, no matter how ridiculous the excuse is. So Bill calls in and tells the boss that he is going to be late because his headlights on the van are not working and he has to wait until the sun comes up to drive into work.

I am sure they recorded this reason and let him come in late. But they will use it against him at the time of cutbacks. I still chuckle at that one!

It is so hard to stay focused at a company that makes you lie to keep your job. It is like going into politics. People love to hear the lies, they want them, which is the reason the phrase truth hurts came about. Reality has to hit you in the head once in a while just to keep you on track.

Really now, the next time you go into work, really listen to what is being said in the way that policies have to be carried out. The only time the truth can be said is when a physical action needs to be fulfilled. IE put that bolt into the hole and tighten it to so many torque pounds.

Let's face it, we lie to keep our jobs we lie to keep our relationships together. We lie to our co-workers and friends. But why do we have to? I have never been able to figure that one out. You borrow money from a friend, and you have all the good intentions at the time of borrowing to pay it back. However you just let it slip away and hope they never ask for it. Now this is a lie, "OH I WILL PAY YOU BACK" so the false promise goes. Hell our own currency is not worth what it says. Is not this a lie, if the dollar bill says one dollar, should it not buy a dollars worth of product? How many times have you heard a politician say the same story again and again, just to get re-elected. And they never do what they say. It does not matter which official is running or for what seat he or she is running to fill. They use the TELL'EM ANYTHING philosophy, just as long as you do not tell them the truth. That is if you want to get elected anyway. Tell the truth and you are back washing dishes and your opponent is the next mayor or president.

INTERNAL DEALINGS

Now here is something that everyone has to deal with when it comes to the corporate structure or laws, or maybe it is just policies? I guess one of the most violated policies is sexual harassment. Oh god can I hear it now, every feminist and equal rights activist is going to trash me on this one. Every corporation nowadays has some type of sexual harassment training and the laws against such actions taken against any employee.

First let me state in my defense, anyone can do any job they want, if they qualify for the position. I do not care and neither does the company you work for. If you are qualified and have put your time in, you should be considered for the position that you applied for, Especially if it is an internal promotion. Can a woman lift a bag of cement? This is a question that is asked dealing with physical limitations that woman are confined to. My answer to that is YES! But why would she want to if there was a man standing there trying to act macho for her. Why would she not let the guy do it? This is being proactive, take that same guy, and if he wanted to lift a bag of cement that is his choice but me I would put it in a wheel borrow. That is just working smart, and if the woman knew that, that man would lift that bag of cement just to prove that he was better than she. She is most certainly not going to stand in his way. Why would she? It is his problem if he thinks that a woman is going to take his job or show him up. This is not true, what is true is that men are so afraid of losing their balls in the face of a woman that he will go out of his way to prove that he is thinking with his balls instead of his brains. He should have said it is your bag of cement, let the woman carry it and then bought her a drink with the gang after work. Maybe I'm wrong on this but, isn't that the reason she took that job in the first place!

It is the same in the offices of corporate head quarters. Work harder at getting the man to do the work she does not want to but yet make it look as if she is doing the job. Now men have to be careful in the arena, because women think differently than men do. A woman can get the job done just as well as a man. But women will get a lot of others to do little parts of the job while the man will try and do it all himself. Both projects get done on time and both projects are as good as the other. But the woman is a little more satisfied because she holds the key. If the man gets the project, he is patted on the back and told a job well done. A woman however is patted on the back and told that she too has done a good job. With a, "I cannot believe YOU beat out so and so on that project". When in reality she was the smart one, she got the input that was needed and she did it right. But we still see her as cooking dinner and cleaning up after us men. And in a man's world, it is war and there are no prisoners just losers and the prize is the woman. The female of the species has never had to battle on these terms before. She can dress in a sexy way but yet present a professional look. If she does it right she can use her sexuality to better her position within the corporate structure. And I do not mean sleep with the boss. All she has to do is give the impression that she will. But if he makes a move on those body suggestions, she closes the sexual harassment clause on him and she still has the position or a lot of hush money awarded by the courts or the company. And that in my opinion is what she wanted in the first place.

If you do not believe me, try telling a woman to dress in a suit and not wear make-up. Who is she wearing it for anyway? Her boy friend or husband is not around so who cares? Why does she wear those skirts that are so short she cannot sit in front of you. If she was there for business then do not distract the client from the business with clothing of such nature. However that is how she gets the client to come aboard the company. Now the company loves this because they get the business and sometimes in a short period of time. So what we have here is a double-edged sword that everyone knows about and uses but no one is allowed to say anything. Because some politician or right winged fanatic says you can't. It would cost more money to tell the truth than to lie, So the lie goes on, and it gets bigger and bigger.

There is a woman or a girl that I worked with, that anyone in the company had no doubt she was a knock out. But we cannot say that to her face because she is the type that would yell sexual harassment that very second. She would wear clothes that are more see through and still fall within the dress code. However the dress codes in the company are more geared toward men than women.

This one day everyone was busting their butts to get a job done. It was weeks in the making and everyone pitched in. The payoff was programs from the company, and it was the hottest and the latest version, a very nice deal. Well the time came and it was kudos for everyone. The software company came and started the handing out of software. There were over 90 people in this process. So we stood in line and took our turns as our time came. Well this woman thought that she should not have to stand in line, so she pushed her way to the front of the line and most of the men thought it was cute. Me however did not let her pass, I told her that I was just as important as she and my work was also just as important. She looked me in the eye and told me she could careless. I told her that if she cut ahead of everyone without waiting her turn I would bust her to the boss. Well she did and so did I. I went up to my boss and told him what she had done, his response to me was "OH DO NOT BE SO HARD ON HER SHE HAS HAD A ROUGH LIFE!" I was left in a pool of wasted human flesh. She had knockers and I didn't. She had jumped from one lap to the next working her way up the ladder. But there was a silver lining. She could not get over the hurdle of our corporate manager. Who happened to be a woman! And I tell you, when a woman has the power over a prettier one, justice is always served.

Now I must confess at this time, if I had her looks and was in her position, I would use everything at my disposal to climb that corporate ladder also. But what we both do not or did not realize, no matter how hard you try or work or wheel and deal or even sell yourself. You will never get to the person who calls the shots.

The only way you can achieve that position is to take your experience and do it yourself. But that is for another section of this book.

Now that I have totally irritated you about the truth of sexual harassment, we can move on to other idiotic things that your bosses and or managers do to keep their positions and not to make waves.

It was told to me time and time again. The definition of Insanity is to do the same thing and expect different results. This to me is good advice. If you are not going anywhere within your position, either change it or do something different to make it better. But do not complain about it. I hate complainers that are not willing to complain to the correct person or even willing to try to fix the problem. Most of the people that have been with a corporation for a long time do not complain. The reason is simple they have become the system, and now they know how to get around it and make life easy on themselves. They could care less about the person that is having the same problem as they did months ago. It is all part of corporate survival. The company wants people loyal to it even though the company is not loyal to them.

This takes me back to the company that I told the man that the sky was blue. It was good times now that I look back on it. I lost that job because I thought it was the greatest job in the world. Until I entered the building to start work, I could not believe that in the interview they told me about this benefit and that bonus. I was hooked; I knew I had the job most people in that little town wanted. Hell they all told me so, and I believed them. It was a de-humanizing job, no brains needed. So down the tubes I went, and I did it faster and better than anyone around. I should have known, the company had an alcohol rehab program for some of their older employees. Now this is taking care of their personnel. But in reality it was keeping a work force alive to run the machines. I was young and fresh and so was a buddy of mine, which we met at the interviews. We brought to the company something they were not expecting or ready for. And that little problem was drugs. Lets face it the next youngest person working in the shop was 10 years older than us. We had a different out look on life. We were taught with new ideas and new ways of doing things. We were thrown into the pit of the old ways. Either conform or quit. But what we choose was not to conform and not to quit. We decided to party as hard and as much as we could to take the pain away. The pain was taking that job and listening to everyone else tell us how lucky we were. We were called the animals, by the front office. It was one of the ways of dealing with our situation. No one wanted to be there, you could tell. Even the foreman was wasted in the shitter before the night was through. Let's face it, the money was good but the job sucks the royal one.

I guess most positions within corporate America delivers the same results. In the military one of the standing rules or is it the unwritten rule, that if you were not bitching then you were not happy. It is how most companies deal with employees. There is no way a company or person can please everyone, especially in a corporation that have large numbers of employees in which to contend with.

The book "ART OF WAR" by Sun Tzu was written some four thousand years ago and suggests the best way to handle multitudes of people is to keep them passive, uneducated, and in fighting. Now the degree of each state depends on the degree of control that is needed. If you are in a battle or in a war the rules from this book apply. You just need to know how to apply them. And yes if you do not know the rules, they still apply only that your competition knows the rules and you do not.

Example: you can have BA and BS degrees and still not know a darn thing that is happening around you in the corporate war. However you could have never finished school and still control power within a corporation, if you knew how the rules of war are applied.

Do not get me wrong, it is war and with it comes every element of war. They have their generals and officers and soldiers. There are battle plans, and strategies and execution of those plans. There will be casualties and heroes, awards will be given and honors bestowed upon the fighting people. It is said as speeches are given telling great tales of how one valiant soldier gave all to achieve this highest honor that can be given to an individual within the ranks. The soldiers cheer and they are motivated to produce more and take the corporation to higher goals and margins. We charge the enemy without fear. Our hearts soar with pride as our CEO rides his white horse into victory.

Ah, the thoughts that makes things great. Motivation is very important within the corporate structure. You must not alleviate it in anyway. Every Corporation knows this and every corporation uses it to the maximum effect. It is the best way to keep employees happy and working toward the best interest of the company. It is funny how the double standards always apply. It has been said many times to me over the years "DO AS I SAY NOT AS I DO" this is an interesting statement. The reason that it is so interesting is it under minds the entire infrastructure of the company, even if the managers who are saying it do not realize what they are saying. Every parent knows that a child learns by doing and seeing what the parent does. Very seldom does a child learn by what the parents told them. It is the same in the work force. People are not stupid even if the management and the company want them to be. But the corporations keep forgetting that employees are smart. The problem is they're at the mercy of the company. The employee has a family and is trying to keep that family going. For this reason the company has the power over the employee and the employee gives the company the power over him. Do you really think, that anyone of you reading this book right now would stay at your place of employment if you had a million dollars? I don't think so. So if that last statement is true then the statement before it is also true. You have to deal with your situation the best that you can or the best that you were taught. The reason the managers are a do as I say and not as I do mental case, is because they were taught that once you became manager you had the power over the new employees who have not learned the system or the internal workings of the company. So if you were a lazy employee and did not organize yourself then you will be a poorly organized manager. Everyone under you will become just like you or the person that is over them, "IF YOU DO NOT CARE WHY SHOULD I?" This will be the attitude of the people under you.

Now for a rude awaking to the managers of the company. The company loves you because you keep the troops working and doing their appointed jobs. But if you think you will ever climb above the status of executive manager or maybe VP, etc. You have another thing coming. Very seldom, and yes there are exceptions to the rule, will a manager achieve the position of true authority within a corporation. The only way a manager will advance to a higher position is to leave the company and apply for the higher position at another organization. The reason for this is credibility; if you start from the bottom the higher ups will always see you as a bottom dweller. For you sarcastic bunch that will say I am full of it. Prove me wrong! I have seen it, I have been there, and no one will admit to it but it does exist. They tell you that you can climb as high as you like or willing to climb, just as long as you do not try to climb over me. Let me move into a story that tells you just how management looks at and deals with lower class employees. I am sure everyone will relate to this one.

Not so many weeks ago, I was placing an order for computer systems with the company that I worked for. It was a sales position, doing corporate sales to other companies. It was telemarketing on a grander scale, but telemarketing nonetheless. I am one to always try and pay attention to details. However there are times in everyone's life that you fall by the way side now and then. Anyway I had placed this order and it was a big one, lots of cash for me in the pocket. The order was placed and then the next day I tracked it to make sure the products were going out. Well I discovered that one of the systems were mixed up and did not ship. Well I had to eat the difference and give the client a scanner out of my own pocket. I was told that I did not pay attention to detail. And since it was my mix up I would take it in the backside. Well I blew up and we argued the good fight. What I did not know at the time, there was no way I was going to win. The reason is someone had to pay for the scanner, and there were three choices. THE CLIENT, THE COMPANY, OR ME now guess which one had to pay. Go figure huh! Well it was not so much as that I had to pay for it, it was the way they went about doing it. First the system that I placed the order on defaulted the price to zero. My defense was this; I, being an account rep, could never enter a price of zero for any product into the system. It would have to be done by a manager. So my question is, if I could not do it why should I pay for it. Well that did not work. They fell back on why did you not pay attention to detail.

Now let me bring the story a little more into focus. Within the sales environment all sales people have to work territories. Which is fine and it is fair to all who work within this group of rules. However there are exceptions to the rules. I was working the east coast and doing real well at it. After a few months of doing and growing my book of clients the company decides that the new group of training sales associates should work the east coast and the team that I was on would move to the central division. Which of course was a tougher market. However they did say we could keep our twenty top accounts. "That was fair", I thought to myself. Time passed and the situation above had come about and the yelling and screaming ensued. I do have a philosophy, if you are going to make an example of me; you better make sure you have your facts straight. Otherwise I will put you in your place in front of the same people you were trying to make the example for. I will admit to mistakes and apologize, but I will not take the blame for someone else, especially if it is someone who thinks that they can push the blame on others. Ok now the set up, Our team was selected to Beta test a new program for the company and then give a report. One of the programs was a faxing program, which would allow faxes to be sent from within the system, or from anyone's computer. So I am testing it with documents from an old account, which was established on the east coast. So I spend one day configuring the system and the programs to the MIS or the tech person's specs. And I sent the fax, are you ready for this?! To our fax machine which was forty feet from my workstation. It was addressed to QOIEKJNFISLS I swear I did nothing but type a bunch of letters. Also I type in big bold letters TEST on the cover page. Just in case the fax went to never, never land, that way no one would mistake it for a real client fax. The following day I walked into the office whistling a happy tune. And slam my manager slaps this fax down in front of me, telling me that this other manager, who really does not care for me in the first place, is yelling at him because his reps are taking account out of territory and this is proof. I was in shock! I first could not believe my manager who was there to protect me from such idiots, and who told me to pay attention to detail. Did not read the fax cover page himself. Or did the other manager, now, if both of them did what THEY SAY, the confrontation would have never taken place. Of course far be it from me not to stand up and make sure the other manager was listening, I yelled out, IF THEY WOULD HAVE READ THE FAX THEY WOULD HAVE KNOWN TO PAY ATTENTION TO DETAILS. It was a small moment of triumph, however small, but you must take them were you can.

Many things occur within the halls of the corporation. Most have to do with image and propaganda. Take for instance, the FOCUS GROUP many companies set up these groups and invite employees to give them their opinions and ideas. The reason that is told is to improve the company and the working conditions within. This however is not the case. How many times has a company looked for ideas from the employees and honestly tried to make it work. NOT OFTEN, why should a company take the ideas of some uneducated flunky who does nothing more than follow the orders that they give. Many times have I worked for a company that have hired people with serious educational backgrounds and have put them into position, which their skills and knowledge mean nothing or just go to waste? I see these brilliant people slowly becoming a mechanism and all the knowledge is gone. While at the same time they hire people off the street to fill a position that one of it's own could fill. However the company does not believe in it's own workers and the workers do not believe in themselves. As a result of this kind of thinking, an educated person bites the dust. There is little that can be done, because the company is not there to teach confidence. The corporation is there to do its service to the community and or it's customers. Now comes the interesting part, in the way a corporation thinks. The standard rule of thumb is that companies love to promote from within. This is true to a point, however I have yet to see a company promote an employee to the position of executive. Now there are exceptions to the rule. But a VP might be as high as you can go. Manager without a doubt is a position that can be achieved. But if you want a higher position in a corporation you will have to move to a different corporation. The new corporation will believe in your abilities to conduct business. The employees will know you are the headman in charge. It comes down to credibility, if everyone knows where you come from, and then they will not take you seriously enough to get the job done. Hell they hate to take orders from you. It is best to go somewhere else. Unless the money is way to good, and how many times have you seen that type of situation?

I hate getting off on tangents, there is so much BS flying around a company it is hard to find your way in the storm. Let me get back to the focus groups, I volunteered for one of these groups. And at first I had high hopes, but that was trashed after the second gathering. First it started out as a get together in the afternoon during work hours. This seemed a good way to change pace from the routine of everyday work.

Our job or objective of the group was to come up with ways to increase productivity and find a way to ease the stress in the workplace. In short, new ways or new ideas to help smooth out the bumps. Seemed good to me, and I was gung ho to get my hands dirty. Then it happened the third meeting changed to after work hours, now I had to stay after and listen to some friend of the Executive tell us how to do and make a good work environment. After which we broke into smaller groups and played an organizational game. This to me was an insult to my intelligent. But the company did not think we had any, so I kept quiet and played the game. The result of the findings was that nothing works because motivation was at an all time low. Now this, to my co-workers and I, did not seem like any earth shattering results. However the executives thought this was a major break through. They stood up and said that we had done a superb job so far, so I quit the next day. And I could not believe the grief that I got from the co-workers who were on the team. "YOU CANNOT QUIT THE GROUP YOU VOLUNTEERED AND YOU HAVE AN OBLIGATION TO FULFILL"! I was shocked at this statement; I looked the person in the eye and said "WHO SAID THAT I CAN'T"? I could not believe it, waste my time with something that is to pacify the employees so that they do not yell to much. When the companies main intention was to divert attention away from what they were doing in other areas of the company. Well the teams went on, they did their duty to the company and sat around these tables of knowledge spilling their thoughts out and acting like they are going to change the mind of someone whom they have never seen. That to me is like someone in another country yelling at a tree because they do not like our way of life. It has no effect what so ever. But these groups must show something for their time and effort. But before I get to that part, I have to tell you about this. The group that I was apart of at one time was to find out why or how the communications was to be done with the phones. This was something that everyone knew about, within the company many years before a focus group was thought of. Well the first step was to acquire a list of all internal numbers in which to look over and find the kinks. This information was disseminated via the intranet within the company. Well the first email hit the desk; it stated that the list was to be reviewed by the leaders of the focus groups first. The group leaders were people that were in the loop at a higher level. So they decided to go over the list to make sure and delete any names and numbers that lower personnel were not allowed to see. So in reality a bogus list was used to fix the problem of the phone list. Now this is the result of great minds. In reality it was a move by the higher ups to keep the lower group members under their control. They were afraid that someone might take their jobs if they knew too much. Everything was geared to look busy, and do nothing that had any effect on the operation of the company and its policies.

Ok here is a group meeting once a week that is controlled by the person that will make the decision as to what was to be reported. Everyone else in the group was window dressing and nothing more. So the couple of months wore on and then it happened. The earth shaking results of the group was published. Or at lease placed on the intranet. It was a two-page report that had a font size ranging from 17 points to 36 points just so it would fill the two pages. It had the names of the team members. It had the vision, it had its goals and objectives, it stated the problem, it stated the steps to resolution, and it had the Solutions.

Are you ready for this? The report suggested, assessing the problem first. Conduct a test and interviews; identify the problems then to create two teams to conduct these suggestions. So if you think about this first part of the three-month focus group, they decide to make two groups to study the problem that the first group was to study.

Second they gave their thoughts on how to proceed or solve some of the problems. AND THE WINNER IS!? Implement a consistent and required standard for ANSWERING THE PHONES AND TRANSFERRING THE CALLS. Oh my god! I could not believe it! They have discovered the heart of why the phones and the 300 employees were having a problem. They did not follow the procedures in the handbook, which was handed out when they got hired. Now this group which wasted the lives of those poor idiots, actually believe that they have accomplished something. Oh I forgot they made suggestions what to do for future projects. Add a job description to the intranet so that everyone will know what they are suppose to be doing, Update the email list, delete unnecessary phone numbers, Correct the phone numbers that were misprinted in the catalog. Now I ask you, does all this seem like a huge waste of time or is it just me? In which none of the ideas, which were presented, which have been around for a while or what I call just plain common sense, will ever be followed up on.

This is either complete stupidity or it is shear brilliance. I watch the people of these groups; they walk around like they have done something important. Now I must say if it gives these people that sense of importance, then maybe the group worked. Everyone needs something to be proud of. I can hardly wait for them to read this book and make the connection to the time when they were in the group.

It is amazing to me that all the crap that can be dumped on you for no other reason than TELLING THEM WHAT THEY WANT TO HEAR. Even when a situation arises that comes to the point of being comical and you can't say a word for fear of reprisal from the idiot that has put you in the situation.

It is like this, a warehouse in any company needs a certain thing to operate properly. The topic of this one particular warehouse is the use of fork trucks. They come in many different styles and types. Each having a good use for what they were designed. Sometimes the truck that is being used is being used for a job that it was not designed for. In this one particular warehouse the racks are stacked five levels. And go back about a pallet and a half deep. Which is well and good if you could use the right truck to maneuver the stock properly. But the truck is limited to its use and operation. To retrieve a pallet out of a location in the warehouse, you race down the aisle looking for the location, you come to a skidding halt. Now I know a lot of you are saying what the hell are you racing down an aisle that is just wide enough for a fork truck and then come to a skidding halt. Is that not dangerous? My response to that is YES it is on the dangerous side. However when the company is yelling faster, faster, get the product out. We are behind schedule, and since they do not have a concern with safety until something goes wrong and someone gets hurt or product is destroyed. All the big wigs come running out yelling why were you not following safety rules. If you tell the truth then you will get fired because they do not want to hear the truth. They want a reason they can tell OSHA so they can keep their jobs. So here comes the shit, no one is going to be blamed but the lowest person on the totem pole. And that is the person busting his ass to get caught up on deliveries, because the company can't afford to hire more people to create a safe work environment. And you want to keep your position with the company so you try to find a scapegoat also. So you "TELL'EM ANYTHING" the brakes on the truck were not working properly. They drag you in to the office and read you the riot act. Threaten to fire you and take away the miserable life, which they have made away from you.

Now here is something that is really interesting to me. You have an accident and the company is all over it with paper. They are yelling and screaming and all the employees are scared shitless. The suits parade around the floor and the rest of the plant with their ties and polished shoes showing everyone that they do not like putting on this show of concern to the lower class people. So for us coming out here, this is what is going through their minds, we will make sure that your lives are hell for the next few weeks, just so that you remember that if you fuck up you will have to see us scare the heck out of anyone in view. So the entire plant makes itself invisible as to not to draw any attention to anyone in particular. It is like when you turn the light on in the kitchen and see all the cockroaches dive for cover. So anyway I was talking to my superior and asked him about the fork trucks and why are we using this type of truck. I told him that we had to use the forks on the truck to drag the pallets as close to the edge of the racks just so we could get a good grip on it without crashing the thing. I asked why we could not get some reach fork trucks with the scissor forks that reaches in and grabs the pallets. This is safer and makes the job more efficient. These trucks could be used in the yard, which would make the yard more efficient. His response to this was, we purchased these trucks and cannot return them. The head office has done a study and found that these trucks are the most economical and most efficient truck on the market. Plus I did a search of all fork truck companies and they agreed with me that these trucks are the best for the job. So under corporate approval I made the decision, that this is the best truck for us and I have not seen another study to dispute the fact. With that he turned and headed to his office. I could not believe he was so blinded to the fact that the trucks were not the right ones for the job. However, it dawned on me that he was the one that made the choice as to which trucks were to be used in the warehouse. Which meant that, if they were not, his ass would be on the line for not being able to make good decisions. So he was not going to cut his own throat just because he made a mistake. So everyone suffered because no one wanted to make waves. Even the head office did not want to hear of problems like this either. One day a few weeks later the fork truck guy was in the plant doing the routine maintenance on the trucks. I came reeling up in my truck and stopped. I hopped off and plugged it in to the wall, to let it power up. I walked over to the guy who was on his knees changing a tire. And far be it from me to let something like an unsatisfactory answer as to why we did something; hold me back from asking more questions.

    I walked up to him asked, how long is our service contract with your company, to service our fork trucks? He looked at me with a questionable look on his face. CONTRACT he questioned? What do you mean? I told him that if we owned these trucks, we had to have hired his company to service them instead of hiring someone to do it ourselves. He looked and said, your company does not own these trucks they lease them from us and I am here to make sure they are kept up and good working order.

I told him that I was told we purchased these trucks and could not return them. I went on to tell the guy about the situation in the warehouse where these trucks were not practical for the job that we were doing. The guy stopped working and sat back on his haunches; he looked at me for a moment then said. "I informed your manager of that a year or so ago. He blew me off so I left it at that". I asked him if his company had the scissor type trucks? He said, "Yes". So I asked him how difficult it would be to swap out one or two of these trucks for the good ones. His next answered stunned me, he said that it was no problem at all. Since we were on a lease they could exchange at any time if they needed to and it would not cost anything to do so. I could not believe what I was hearing. Then the question came to mind, if we could swap out these for the ones that would do a better job, why not? The answer to this came to me in a mean way. It is my fault for pursuing this matter, but it bugs me to see great things or good ideas go to waste because of someone else's pride and ego. I confronted my manager again about the trucks and told him what I was told by the fork truck man. My manager went ballistic, he was yelling at me and jumping up and down, and he put the fear in me because I wanted to see something better for the company. When I think back on it, he knew down inside, to get me to conform he would have to make a scene in front of everyone in the plant and humiliate me in front of everyone. So that is what he did. His yelling and screaming made everyone stop and look at us. No one knew what it was about, because they were all to far away to know. All they could see was the boss man ripping me a new asshole. I buckled up and got on my high horse and rode away. Or maybe it was the fork truck and headed back to work pulling pallets with the stupid truck that this little Hitler for a manager decided was the best one because some higher ups said it was without checking to see if it truly did the job.

Now I did not know at the time how much this festered inside of him. So about a week or so had gone by and I was out on the floor deep in the racks pulling product. When around the corner came the little Hitler dude followed by the higher ups. They had to wait until I was done pulling the pallet, because the aisle was just wide enough for the truck. But the little Hitler wanted the higher ups see me using the truck. I got the pallet down on the floor and turned the truck so they could get by. The little Hitler stops at my truck and says. "WELL I SEE THAT THE DECISION I MADE IN CHOOSING THIS TYPE OF FORK TRUCK WAS A GOOD ONE". All the higher ups turned and looked at me for a response to what was just said. They all had the look on their face that stated you want your job you will answer in the proper way. So I did what everyone else did. "TELL'EM ANYTHING" in a resistive voice, and more under my breath, "yep" that is all I said. With that response the most shit eating smile grew on the little Hitler's face. He had won and his job was safe. He knew he had won because I just validated his position in front of the big wigs. His stock went up and mine went down. Because I was a yes man now, it would be tagged to me as long as I worked there. No matter what I would do to try and change things or give ideas to help make it a better company. It would be shot down and they knew there was nothing that I could do about it. I had empowered the Hitler with my life. And to fight now would be grounds for dismissal. No questions asked and no repercussions on the Hitler dude.

Looking back on those days in hell, I wonder what it was that made me want to save a scum position with a company that did not give two hoots weather I died or lived. They would just get someone else to do the same job. This was one of the first steps that I had to take to becoming a free man and not let anyone run my life, unless I wanted them to. Let's face it any job you take, you have sold your soul to the company for a price. And for that price you will do what they want. Do not make waves, to not think or be creative or give input. Unless they want the input, and your idea or suggestions must be of the type that just look good and that is all.

Just remember one thing, if you are invited to give ideas at a group or any other form. If the head executive is not there or he or she did not ask for it, then it will be filed as propaganda to give the employees a place to bitch. Hardly ever, does anything come out of these groups or suggestions. If they do not pay you for it, why should you do it? Hell these companies hire people to do that very thing. So why would they need your input, unless it is to make you think you are important.

Dealing with people on the inside is tough. It happens all the time, just when you think you know a person, bam, they change. This happened yesterday on the job. We as a company were changing out monitors on our computers. Not a difficult job, however there was and always will be someone who cannot follow instructions no matter how simple. This is the rule and it will always be the rule. Well the instruction was to write the number of the monitor on the SIDE of the box, and that box was to be placed with the number to the outside so the movers can read the number. Seems simple enough, but, and yes there is always a but; one of the teams wrote the number on top of the box. Well as in all mistakes the manager walks up just as he finishes writing the number on the box top. Our manager who I thought was a good guy and tried to be the perfect boss showed his real colors. He flew off the handle and proceeded to make our co-worker an example and put him down at the same time. He was pissed because no one would do what he wanted! He was mad because the team did not show him respect. He was pissed because no one would listen to him. He let all this pent up anger out in front of everyone and directed it a fellow worker. This is one of the basic cardinal rules that should never be broken.

Here is a man that wanted the world to look up to him, but what he found was, when you look down on everyone, it makes it very hard for them to look up to you. He has not learned the ways of people. The more you apply pressure and tighten your grip the more they fight and squeeze between your fingers. He continues to recite a passage or motto, it goes like this THE DEFINITION OF INSANITY IS WHEN YOU DO THE SAME

THING OVER AND OVER AGAIN AND EXPECT A DIFFERENT RESULTS. I think this is a very good motto, however he does not realize that he is doing the same thing over and over again. He always says the same thing, the only difference is that he is getting louder and louder. I sort of feel sorry for him. I want to help him out but he does not want the help and he really believes that he knows everything. I was blinded to his ways, now don't get me wrong, I am as much of a kiss ass as the next person. But he takes it to extremes. His letters to the VP's are dripping with lip balm. He thinks he is being so smart and coy, yet everyone sees just what he is doing. He will learn, the higher ups will use him until he is needed no more. Then they will put him out in the trash with the other used items of the company.

Now here is a strange turn of events, I just got home from work. My manager took me aside and gave me a speech. He recognized that if he does not please me or find out what is wrong, I will infect the team spirit and he will not be able to achieve his own goals. I don't want to sound like I am some kind of evil person that is out to destroy the world around him. But I must tell you that if you know yourself and know other people and their actions, you are in a much better position in life. You do not have to have the title or position to be in charge. If you are the most respected on the team or in the company the others will follow your lead. Warning you can loose your job if you over step your bounds in this area. The key to success is to not let them know you are the one controlling the situation. Many leaders have been puppets for unseen controllers. Many management positions are the same thing; they are front people for the real men and women of power.

To give an example of what I am talking about. Let us take a look at the movie industry. Everybody loves the actors and actresses on the big screen. Even with all the notoriety the actors still are not happy. They all want to direct and produce the films why is this? The reason is, they are not in control, they are told what to do, when to do it, and where to do it. You see a puppet of someone else's ideas. All performers want to be in control. We as people are always fighting for control of our lives. We always want to be someone else, act like someone else, and have the things of others. What we do not see is the other people looking at us wanting the things we have. THERE IS ALWAYS SOMEONE BETTER OFF THAN US, PLUS THERE IS ALWAYS SOMEONE WORSE OFF THAN US. You must recognize this if you ever want to progress in the world of corporate survival. Now to continue with what happened today! My manager pulled me aside to have a talk about what was happening to the team. Our team morale has gone to hell real fast. He is a self-centered person who tries to take credit for others. He asked me what I thought was going on with the team. He told me a few things that are going on with the team. To give an example he told me his side of the story about the shitty bus ride and firing of the employees afterwards. He told me that the employees that were fired were fired before they got on the bus. He told me that they knew it and they had a choice. Go home and pick up their checks later or take the trip and pick up their checks after. He told me that they knew they were being let go. Then he played on my heartstrings, which is one of the hardest things anyone has to deal with. He told me he had to come into the break room to regain composure, because it hurt him so deeply. He told me his wife had to console him because of his pain. He then made a slip of the tongue; he told me that he has been doing this for fifteen years. My question is this, if he has been doing corporate dealings for fifteen years, he shouldn't have had such a hard time with firing people. He just didn't want to be the bad guy, and the company made him do the dirty work. I must say he is learning the trade, but he wanted the title and he didn't think it would cost him anything. His tongue slip told me that he wanted to know how I was doing what I was doing. The day he knows the answer to that question will be the day he does not have to ask it. RESPECT is the number one reason that managers fail or succeed at their positions. Most managers don't even know the meaning or even where to find it. It is funny, I told him at this meeting that he has to show some respect to get the respect. I also said that it might be a good place to start getting the team back on track again. However, he told me that if the team wants respect they must first show him respect. But the only rule respect has is you have to earn it. It cannot be given to you like a gift. I don't know if he will ever learn this but he is trying. He is also looking to me to fix his team, and I have to say that I cannot help him if I keep getting the short end of the stick.

Oh one other thing we talked about, which is the chewing out of one of the other employees. I talk about this in another chapter. I told him when he flew off the handle and bawled the guy out in front of everyone; he really blew it with the team. I told him that he might have to apologize to the guy, which if he does he will win the respect of the team. He told me he would not apologize and that it was good to humiliate him. It would teach him a lesson. His argument was that he had a boss who did it to him and it taught him a big lesson. Well I can tell you that he is becoming that very boss he hated. No one needs to be humiliated at work just because you wanted to teach someone a lesson. It takes a big man to apologize and still be in charge, his refusal to apologize just shows how weak he really is. I tried to tell him and he did the very thing that he hates. He did not listen! He thinks he is better than the rest of us, just because he knows more information on the situation in the company does not make him a better man. He holds information, as it is a secret to be kept from others.

Yes information on operation of an organization is important to be given to certain people for the purpose of focusing the company. However information withheld that directly affects a person, just for the sole purpose of gaining power over someone, will come back and bite you in the ass as it did with my manager.

Hello, it is the next day and I must say it has been one interesting solar rise and fall. When I arrived at work today, every boss person was lined up at the front door like a gauntlet. They were clapping and doing the high five to everyone that came in. Now this was a direct response to the meetings that were conducted the day before. I could see that they were trying to rebuild the morale that they destroyed in the first place. I must say it did help some but the mistake that they made was, they did not keep it going. They did it and went right back to the old ways of doing business. However they expected the world to change.

Later on they or my manager called an emergency meeting. We all went in and laid our shit on the table and he did the same thing. However he took up our points of view and ideas and twisted them to fit into his way of thinking. He has not learned that it is not about HIM, he continues to say I did this and I did that, and you never do anything I want. I do not think he will learn.

CYA
COVER YOUR ASS

Now here is a chapter that I think everyone relates to. Covering your ass at work has got to be one of the highest priorities of any employee that wants to climb that corporate ladder. CYA should be the MISSION STATEMENT of most corporations in America these days.

For some odd reason I have always liked this statement. Cover Your Ass! Yes everyone knows it and everyone talks about it. But how many people really do it? You sit there thinking that the company and the people that run it are good all American people. They were raised and brought up just like everyone else; they have the same values and morals as everyone else. The answer to that is YES they do. If you were their friends and partner working together to build a corporation, all of the above it true. But if you think that they care as much about you as they do their own families. You better think again! Let's look at it like this, you are working hard to build a family and a life. You want the best for your family. You want to see your children grow up and become successful in life. What would you say if the owner of the company that you worked for died? Your first thoughts in your mind would be, are they going to close the plant? What will happen now? Will I have to find another job? Then maybe you might say I feel sorry for MR. BIG BOSS. But you really don't feel sorry for him; you just want to make sure you have a paycheck the next week. Covering your ass is very important. The company does a lot of things to build a case against the employee, just in case they have to fire him or her in the future. Do you really think that all the record keeping that is done on you is for your sake! Look at what they keep track of, how often are you late? What is your work performance like is it bad or good? They have you fill out statements that will be used against you weather you fill them out or not.

For instance at this one company, they have us fill out daily reports as to what we have accomplished in the days work. Some of the things you cannot get to in a reasonable time. Sometimes you can, but the question on the report states, did you do this or that? And the answer is either yes or no. Your supervisor explained to us that it did not matter just as long as you turned the reports in and did them honestly. So at the time of turn in the manager says that is ok. I know what you were doing at the time and I know why you did not get to this project or that one. But they do not enter it into the report. This is where the problem resides. It is over a period of months and then something happens were they question your work performance. They pull the report and look at it, it was a bad day and then they ask what the hell were you doing on this day? You have nothing to back you up. It is simple as that. It is done everyday in every business in America and around the world. They tell you it is for you, and then they use it against you. Do not be fooled, always keep a separate record for yourself, and make copies of everything they have. Also you have the right to see your records. So once a month demand to see them and check to see what is in your file. Check to see what they are saying about you. Never ever believe them when they tell you they are confidential! Who's records are they anyway, and yes they have used that one on me before. I can understand if I wanted to see another person's records, but not being allowed to see my own. I do not think so; I went straight to human resources and demanded to see my records. Yes they can have someone with you. But they cannot keep the records from you. If they do, a phone call to the employment office will change their minds real fast. It is your right to know what kind of records the company is compiling against you, and you have the right to dispute any allegations that they might have or say against you.

    It is a tough world out there and everyone is trying to make a life for him or herself. Just to let you know how much the company cares, I will tell you what happened to some friends or co-workers I use to work with. It was the factory and everyone thought the job was permanent. Some of these guys were doing the same job for well over twenty years. They gave their heart and soul to the company and even put some serious money away in the pension fund for when they retired. I quit the job because who wants to be the one known as "THE ONE THAT FLEW

OVER THE FACTORY" it was the only way they knew how to handle my situation with overdosing on drugs. So I use to hate them for that, but they were more scared of becoming like me than they were scared of me. They saw their future, in my over dose, they all thought they were heading down the same path. I hate to say it but many were on the road to down fall.

So these guys gave everything, their body and soul, breathing that cast iron dust six days a week, just to make the extra money then drinking it or smoking it on the weekends. Well I left, and none to soon. I got a letter from a friend stating that the plant closed and everyone was out of a job. The old timers lost their pension or most of it. They gave everything to the company and the company sold out. Sure enough the owners got their stash, but the workers were out. Not even a thank you. Now the company that purchased the building, opened about a year later. Just enough time to make the people desperate for work, most of the old employees tried to get in and some did at smaller wages this time doing almost the same job. However the old timers were not hired because they were ready for retirement and the company did not want to pay the retirement, besides they wanted young people so they would stay with the company for twenty years so they can do the same thing to them.

I have seen this same scenario three times in my trek across the country. I could not believe that no matter what part of the country I was in the corporate rules and policies were always there. They read different and sounded different but they were all basically the same.

It is funny how they make it sound like the company is for the workers and how many workers really believe it. But they the workers are fooling themselves; a great motivator told me, that the best time to look for a job is when you don't need one. I have done so and have climbed the ladder and even owned my own company. And yes the rules applied at my corporation also.

It is so important to COVER YOUR ASS at any position you take no matter how high up the corporate ladder you are. Everyone is trying to climb that ladder and they will tear you down if they can just so they can get up there. It is like a game of KING OF THE HILL, everyone fighting to get to the top. But only one can stand on top until he or she is knocked off. So even the owner of the company can be dethroned. However he or she can jump off with the goods and go somewhere else to play.

There are many things that you have to be on guard against. One of the main things is the SCAPEGOAT PHILOSOPHY, which if you have ever worked for any corporation for any length of time, you would have seen the indicators of this philosophy. It comes in to play at the moment something goes wrong. It does not matter what the problem is either, they do not care what caused it or why it is happening. They just want someone to blame for the situation. Not all the time but most of the time the person that ends up being fired or using the nice words LET GO, will be an employee who was following the rules or orders of his or her superior. Corporations work under a view that our government works. They do not believe that problems happen over a period of time. They believe it was an isolated incident, which can be solved by finding the closest person to the problem, and this person must not have much importance within the corporation, then make that person the scapegoat. They will make sure the entire corporation's employees see and know what happened and why this person is being let go.

This is the foundation of COVERING YOUR ASS, if you do not you will become the scapegoat. What is sad in my eyes is that if the people of a corporation would focus on how to do something instead of trying to find fault with everyone and everything, companies would run smoother and make more profit and even the employees would stay longer and work harder for the company. The main thing you have to look at is, people are people. We never give them a chance or never allow a mistake or a chance to correct the mistake. Everyone makes mistakes, however if they make the same mistake twice, GOOD BYE, then it becomes a cost factor. But most of the time it is an ego factor and management is looking to feed it's own ego. Adding another brick in the wall, I always loved that album by PINK FLOYD, it says so much. I have always wondered if that is what the album was intended or was it a fun record to make, some day I should ask them.

You have to be on the lookout for managers that are bullies and have no management skills what so ever. It is easy to spot these people, they are afraid of their own shadow and the shadow of the executives. The executives love these types of people and managers, they are mean and yell a lot. They manage by intimidation; they do not care who is right or who is wrong. They want a head or ass to roll or chew. When they do their thing they want to make sure the higher ups see it or know about it. After the deed is done the executive will pat their dog on the head and give him a good boy. These people are not limited to men only, they come in the women form also.

The funny thing about the pit bull manager is he or she really thinks they are making a difference within the company. But in reality they are bitch dogs of the executives. They are first to yell but the last to ask for anything, which will help the company, or the employees perform their jobs better. I must say, managers like this are important to the corporation. These people are not afraid of anyone who is under their command. However if you stand up to them and voice your opinion, they will fold fast and go running to the executive with their tail between their legs for protection.

In real life these managers have no life and they want to make sure they are the ones that keep others from having a life. They are paid just enough to keep them doing their job and awarded enough not to question what is asked of them. They have no ambition or goals to strive for. They think they are in charge of their own destiny but are scared to look in the mirror. They would never question the chain of command, even if the chain needs to be questioned.

If you are a true manager, and, the executives want a true manager, yes they do want one or two working within the structure, but these are guarded position, because the true manager will become a threat to their position within the corporation. They do not want to loose their spot on the ladder to someone beneath them. However a good manager that knows how to manage is the one that keeps things running smooth when all else is chaos. These are the people to find and learn from.

So the question to me is, how do you find the good manager within the company? That is one of the easiest questions to answer. Just watch to see which manager the employees go to, to solve problems. He or she will always have people around them that need answers. He or she will also be the one that all the other managers talk about, in a semi-negative way. They all know this person is a mover and shaker, and they are jealous of this person. Oh let me say this, any manager that reads this book and tells me that I am full of shit. You are the one that has become the bitch dog of the company. The reason for this is a good manager knows he or she is a good manager and is not afraid of competition or criticism. Oh another note on this, these statements will not even affect a good manager. Because they also know that they are on the climb to better places and have no need of petty jealousy from bitch dog managers. I know of one bitch dog manager who thinks he is the greatest thing since sliced bread. What he refuses to see, and the reason why I say refuses to see, is because there is enough said about this guy and the way he treats his team or department, that even he cannot be shielded from the fall out. He has been told to his face that he is a pain in the ass. He does not believe it, and continues as always. However he does get pissed when his own department goes to a different manager for advice. He walks around like he has a corncob stuck up his ass. He will never make eye contact with anyone. Which is the sign of weakness and non-respect to others.

This one month my manager who is ambitious and a good manager, just naïve to the ways of the corporate life, he thinks he can change the system to run the way it says in the books. So this month rolls around, now I was not at the meeting so the only thing I can do is speculate as to what went on in this meeting. These two managers got into a ego match who was better or whose team was the best. It was a civil meeting and no one got punched out. The bet was whose team ever had the best GP (gross points) at the end of the month would buy the other team pizza at Pizza Hut the next week. The month wore on and through the entire month our team was lagging. Everyday it was a stress factor on our manager. Myself, and the rest of the team knew he was under the gun. He was a good manager as I have said before, however he had a habit of speaking without thinking. He was new at the game and wanted to make his mark in the world. He was up against stupidity and arrogance, so he would walk around with this look of "save my ass" on his face. Day in and day out the numbers came in and dog bitch's team would beat us. And the depression would deepen. His hair was turning gray right before our eyes; to me this was way over the edge for achievement. This guy was going to have a heart attack over a dog bitch. Who was his equal on the scale of corporate officers, it is not worth it. But we as a team liked him so we tried to do our best to help him out. There were things that were against us; first thing is the dog bitch came into management from the floor. So he had cultivated good clients, which he gave to one of his team. He also treated the rest of his team like shit. So it was his best man against us. Now this one person was a damn good sales person and could get the numbers if needed. He was the dog bitches ace in the hole. He had continually beaten our team in numbers from the start. So the dog bitch knew he had it in the bag. Second our manager came from training and all his accounts were distributed along time ago before he became a sales manager. Also more than half of the team was brand new people. There were only four of us who were strong sales people. And out of the four, only two were making any type of GP. I was one of them, but my attitude sucked because of commission dollars they took away. I won't go into that in this chapter. So that really left one against one. Now the lady that was the number one on our team, had brought her clients from another company to this one. She was doing well, however most of her clients were gone on vacation. It was a freaky thing, which was no big deal, except to our manager who made the bet. Well the pressure was on, he was looking for ways to get me motivated and back on my horse to save him. He was hovering over the rest of the team, trying to get them up to speed. It seemed nothing was working. The month wore on and on, and there was no hope in sight. Then a saving grace came to our top girl. She got a call from one of her clients that she had not talked to in awhile. They wanted somewhere around one hundred licenses for some software. She was excited and our manger was excited.

Everyone was calculating how much GP it was worth. All they could figure that it was going to be close. But the gap was a huge one.

I swear to god I thought our manager was giving birth or something. He was pacing and waiting until the numbers were in. Then it happened! The tally sheet came out and we had creamed the other team. Our top girl and our manager figured the GP wrong and it put us over by more than two thousand GP points.

It was party time! The stir that it created was incredible, and boy did the shit fly. What was interesting about this is the employees of the teams were cool to each other. As a matter of fact I did not know we won until one of the other team members congratulated me. I thought now that was great. We our team of course gave the top girl the credit for doing a good job. Then it started, the bitch dog was pissed and he did not take this well. He started to complain to the higher ups. Even though they did not have anything to do with it. However they gave the bitch dog ideas on how to change the rules of the contest. He started to pull numbers of returns or non-credits. He started to deduct the points from our team. After he was done his team was the winner. And the bitch dog made sure that everyone on our team knew we did not win. It turned into a bitch match, which should have never happened. It dragged the chain of managers into it and everyone was trying to solve the issue. It was blown way out of proportion. It was a friendly bet between two teams, and if the bitch dog won nothing would have been said, but he lost and he did not like that. He did everything in his power to make sure he did not look like the loser that he was. Well to this day it was never settled and I know it was dropped, just because he cried all the way to the top. You know as well as I that top executives hate shit like this and told everyone to shut up. Now let me tell you what this did for the bitch dog. He lost all respect from his team and his numbers have been declining ever since. It created animosity between him and other managers. Not to mention the animosity between the employees of the teams that were involved. This is what happens when you change the rules for self-preservations. He is the type of person that would cut off his nose to spite his face. It is hard to deal with people of this nature. But deal with them you must, you will find that in the process of dealing with them, they will end up dealing with you. What I mean by that is at first you have to put up with their shit, until you find out that their shit isn't worth it. You will kick yourself after this little discovery but you will get over it and continue on with your life. They or the dog bitch manager will continue with his way of life, and he will continually try to figure out why everyone is passing him up on the way to the top of the ladder. All the while he is being treated like a bitch dog. I've got news for him, he will never figure it out and there is no sense in telling him because he would not listen to an underling, which is the only time you have to deal with him anyway. So forget him you are the most important person in your life. If you think that any company really cares about your welfare then you need a good kick in the ass. No company cares more about their employees, than it does of its own existence. A corporation is a person and it will try to survive at all cost. Just remember in a crisis situation an employee is the first casualty.

What is that I hear, the voice of morality? Did someone say that is not so? The only time morals ever made a difference in money making decision is when you are donating to a charity. Even then the choice will be made so it will benefit the person making the donation. And again prove me wrong! I have no problem being wrong, what I do have a problem is, when people say they are doing it out the kindness of their hearts. That is such bullshit. When you give money to a person on the street, is that act an act of kindness from your heart or is it guilt because you have something that you worked hard for and they didn't. If you see someone on the street with a sign will work for food, ask him or her what he or she is selling. Check to see if it is employment for compensation of food or is it just and easy way to get money? What am I talking about? When you enter the interview for the first time. You ask certain questions and you answer certain questions. What am I suppose to do for the money you will pay me? They will tell you what is expected and then they will expect you to do it. So if someone wants money from you, what goods or service is that person supplying. Oh I am sorry, was this question supposed to be in the supply and demand chapter? It is all the same thing. You must COVER YOUR ASS, if you give that guy a buck what do you expect in return for that dollar. If you say a feeling of goodness, I'm going to slap you, because you are TELLING THEM ANYTHING or what you think they want to hear. The truth being is if they hold that sign in your face long enough you will feel guilty and give them a buck. Then you hit the gas on your car and get out of the situation as fast as possible. Want them to leave you alone? You want me to tell you how to make them leave you alone? You do not even have to say a word or make mean gestures. All you have to do is look at them in the eye. It is a staring match, you do not have to look down on them just look at them and do not be afraid they cannot hurt you. They will turn away within forty five seconds. Time it; you will see I am right. The question is are you strong enough to stand your ground when it comes to a buck or will every lazy panhandling person take everything from you turning you into a DOG BITCH MANAGER! It is your choice. No one makes you do the things you do. You make the choices! If you do not have the guts to stake your own claim or make your mark. And you want to do it. Ask the ones that are doing it. They will tell you, they will help you. But if you are not serious and are just looking for ways to use them to climb over them, they will sniff you out and dump you like a bad habit.

As you will see later on in this book there are many situations that over lap each other. It is very important to keep your eyes open to everything that is going on not only with yourself but with fellow employees and middle management also. Covering your ass is the only thing that will give you longevity within the corporation. It is a dog eat dog world and if you think you are safe and secure you had better look again. The key to this battle is to dig your self in deep. Make yourself hard to replace, or dig up dirt so they don't want to replace you. Or there is another option and that is to become their dog bitch and do the dirty work of the company.

I get asked why am I like this? Why do I look at things in this way? My answer to that question is do you want the truth or do you want me to TELL'EM ANYTHING, or something that you want to hear. No one wants to know the truth, and when we do hear the truth, we say oh he was such a nice person, or he always kept to himself. When in reality these very same people that tell us that, never gave two shits about what the other person was doing. They did not want to know that the person or even their own children were doing things that would turn into rage and hurt someone. No you are just like everyone else, you want to have the American dream, a house two cars and 2.5 kids with a dog and a cat. I was talking with my manager the other day. The topic of discussion was the mass firings that took place that week. He wanted to know how I felt about what was going on. I asked him did he want the truth or some story? He told me THE TRUTH, so I told him that I though it was a shitty thing to do. Not in the firing, but in the way they did it. He immediately stated, well it is not what you think. I stopped him, and told him that he wanted to hear the truth from me. If he wanted a story he should have said so. My thinking on this is he was looking for information on the situation and I was not looking for an excuse to why they did it; so don't offer a false story to me. It is true that if you plan to worm information out of someone, be prepared to have your plans uncovered. If you are not ready then your credibility will be ruined, and the person you were trying to get information from will make sure that all within earshot will know what you were trying to do. This type of information gathering is done on all levels of business. Just be on the look out for the gathers of the company. Yes you will know them and can spot them, or your co-workers will point them out to you. So the reason in my mind as to why I think this way is from the Air Force, they taught me to look at things in a different light. They showed me just the tip of the iceberg as to what propaganda is and how it works. I was privy to tactics used by the military for promoting the American way of life. It was the basics on how information was given to the public, both good and bad. They showed me that bad propaganda was just as effective as good propaganda. They showed the results of different campaigns and how it was disseminated. It was discussed in brief that these tactics could be used in any country or area to achieve an out come of their design. I was in awe and shock at the same time.

However I was fascinated by it. Not only could our government do such things so could other countries and even corporations. Just bare in mind that anything that can be done on a grand scale can also be done on smaller scales. Looking at the world through rose colored glasses is great for awhile, but some time you must take them off to see what is happening around you. You can look at it like a horse drawn carriage, the master or driver is above looking to see what is up ahead, and he puts blinders on the horse so it only sees what he wants. If he had a horse with no blinders it would see a world that offered other things and the horse would want to head towards greener pastures. The military knows this and that is why in basic training they teach and make everyone the same. Not only is the hair cut a health action; it is also a psychological tactic. No one is better or worse than the person standing next to him. You look the same, you are yelled at the same, you eat and sleep just like everyone else. This is both mental and physical conditioning. The reason for this is when the time comes for the officer to yell charge, the men will charge. If freethinking is instituted into the military, the results are a discussion on whether or not it is a good idea to charge. I know it sounds funny, however if you look at Vietnam, and the stupidity of yelling charge you can see the results. It was like the BOY WHO CRIED WOLF. Back in history at the beginning of the war, the officers would yell charge and everyone gave their best. Then years past and the same person was yelling charge, and the charge was up the same hill that was charged thirty times in the past. The soldiers began to think, WHY ARE WE KILLING OURSELVES FOR THE SAME PIECE OF PROPERTY? They began to question the ideals of the officers. If you are going to use propaganda to get the employees to do something, it will have its effect. However if you use the same speech over and over again, the employees will look at you and laugh. A company who looks at its employees as expendable items will have a crew of non-caring people who will rip the company off the first chance they get. This in turn makes the company clamp down tighter and tighter. This becomes a vicious circle. No one wants to be treated like tomorrow is their last day, or they are the scum of the earth. A good company will use the propaganda to create positive thinking and good feelings within the ranks, even if their intentions are different.

There is a guy who works in the building, he is Mexican and is a nice man. The reason I bring this up at this time is, this man comes around everyday and empties the trashcans at our desks. He is polite and friendly, I talk to him everyday, I even talk to him when he is not empting the cans. Many people at work look down on him and they do not give this man the time of day. If he misses their trash can they yell and scream. He will tell them he is sorry and move on to the next desk. I knew that this man was something more than he was presenting. For my own curiosity I made a point to take an interest in him. I asked him about his job and what he does. He knew that I was interested for the sake of myself and no one else. He read me very well and knew I was no threat to him or is job. So he told me all about the company. He was the owner of the cleaning company and he had serious accounts. He told me he would clear two grand a week cleaning the buildings. I knew he was more than he appeared. He was making more money than the top sales people who were mean to this man. He would look at these arrogant people and just smile. He did the: I don't speak English thing with them, and went his own way.

What a great man he is, and I do mean great. He was not caught up in the politics of the day. I am sure he had to do the boss man thing for his own employees, however he was in the trenches with the workers who were under him.

I cannot believe the bullshit that is pilling up at work. I must bring this to your attention since something new happens everyday on the job. It is a Monday; I was in early like I always am. NOTE: this is from experience, and I know many of you will attest to the fact, if you go into work early and get caught up on work. You are doing the job they hired you for, however, they do not care if you get caught up or if you come in early. You must stay over so they can see you, and know they are getting their monies worth. I have to stay late once or twice a month just to make sure they know I will stay late. However I do absolutely nothing, I make sure that every boss and big shot in the place sees me. It is very important that they see you. Warning: if you are one that stays late all the time they will take you for granted. Make sure you go home on time and make it a point to let a few people know you are doing so, make sure your manager knows what time you go home. This will set up the perfect stay late situation. When I stay late everyone comes up to me and makes a joke, OH IS YOUR WATCH BROKEN? Stuff like that, but what they do not know is it draws attention to myself and the big shots notice that I am going out of my way for the company. They will come up to me and say stuff like, WE LIKE PEOPLE WHO GIVE THAT LITTLE EXTRA! What a crock, there are people that bust their asses more than I do and they get shit on by the company just because they are there all the time. The big wigs think that is the time they are suppose to work, so they don't give them any credit for staying late.

There is the guy who sits next to me, and he learned the hard way about staying late. He is hyperactive in the first place, so when this client of his called and needed this great quote, he busted ass on it. He stayed late into the evening to get the quote done, and what he got for his troubles was, sorry we are going with another vendor on the order. No one in the building gave two shits if he stayed late. His clients didn't give two shits either. So I ask you, why should you destroy your life trying to create something good for a company that could care less about it? That is the reason that I am out of there on the dot. They make jokes about it and wonder where I am going all the time. Hell sometimes I come home and sit in the pool. The point is, it is my time and I will do with it as I see fit. This company gave a speech stating that if you make your sales and you can come and go as you please. However they make sure they pound on you every chance they get. It's like the merry-go-round, they continue to hold brass rings out for you to catch. However you miss more than you catch, and the ride never stops. Once you are on the ride, they make it tough to get off. After you tasted the poison of their ideas you being to allow them more and more liberties. Today was a day that will go down in personal history for my manager. I speak well of him throughout this book. As I have said before he is a good man and means well. However he has not yet been burned bad enough to open his eyes to the problems of the waters in which he swims. I knew when I first met him; he had been tainted by visions of greatness. I knew in my heart that he saw himself as president of the company. He also believed that he could become president at this company. Taking the naïve book of hard work in hand he stood his ground. He builds a foundation for himself and taught his beliefs to the new employees of the company. He was on a quest of good honors and ethical dealings in corporate America. Hell, he was even a good man to his fellow employees. However he did have a fault and that fault was he had serious pride in himself and what he was doing. This pride blinded him to what was really going on around him. He thought the company wanted him to build a crack sales team that the industry could be proud of; he wanted us to be put on display for all the world to see.

I did not see it happen but our team was a buzz with the managers meeting that took place today. The main rumor was the words that came out of his mouth. "FUCK THIS PLACE" was the repeated phrase. The toll from all sides this man was taking had to be building for some time. Even as I write these words I know that there is more to come. His threshold has not been breached yet. And knowing the way the company operates. They will not stop until they find his breaking point. Just as all the other mangers did nothing to help in the past, they are all standing around waiting for him to fall.

The courtship of account sales personnel has already started. One of the most despised managers started his sniffing of our team today. They are waiting for the rest of the team to fail and then they will take out our manager and take the best of the team for their own.

All I hear everyday is how we all should be loyal to the company and to each other. We should help one another so we can all profit. What the sad thing is that the person that is saying all this is the one that will loose everything he is trying to accomplish within the company. The reason he is going to loose is because he does not believe the company and his fellow employees are playing a back stabbing game. He thinks everyone is dedicated to the company. He is so wrong, I can see it and so can many others. I have tried to talk to him about what is going on within the company, but he will not listen. It is funny because he has been screwed over three or four times by some of his so-called co-workers and friends and he still takes them at face value. He called me in on a one on one, it was evaluation time, so he takes me into this room and proceeds to talk about how we are friends and that he would tell me if anything was going on. He said that he would tell me because we were friends.

He is so full of shit; he is trying to get information out of me so he can do his job (or is it SAVE his job). He tries twisting the conversation so that it is not he doing the bad things. But it is the company making him do the bad things. To a point he is correct, he just wants to save his ass and he will not defend anyone on the ropes. Here is a corporate warning, if your company brings in a consult to find new ways, to control cost or make the place more efficient, WATCH OUT! This consultant is nothing more than a hatchet man, the company that hires one of these people is a spineless company and has no guts to clean house on their own. Here is the reason why; a consultant is paid good money so the company can cut costs! Now does this make sense? Any company that wants to cut staff should sit down and do it. However they do not want to be the bad guy. With the consultant they can blame the consultant and by the time the smoke clears that person is paid and on their way to the next company. Don't get me wrong; if a company hires a consultant to help with a new advertising campaign or maybe a new product roll out, this is good. However if your company tells everyone that the consultant is there for the reason of efficiency then you better take heed. The consultant is there to cut employees and nothing else. Most companies will hire a hatchet man to cut the staff in order to show a better profit bottom line. As each quarter nears the end, a company will look at the bottom line to see if it looks good enough to present to the stockholders. If it does not come up to the expectations of the stockholders the company has a few options that they can turn to, so that they can justify the bottom line. The most effective way to do that is by cutting employees. People are the fastest way to change a budget or bottom line at any company. It does not have a drastic effect on the work that is produced; it does however dump extra work on the employees that are left standing after the ax is swung.

I just love the way they say stuff like, "THEY ARE HERE TO EVALUATE THE COMPANY." I just wonder to what definition evaluate applies to? If you think that the company gives a rat's ass about you and the position you hold, you better think again, because it doesn't care. Their main concern is making the books look good for the stockholders or IRS or any other organization that is important to the operation of the company.

Well it was that time again where you have to make a showing just to throw them off the track. I know what you are saying! "WHAT THE HELL IS HE TALKING ABOUT"! Well it is like this, as you can tell this book is written from past experiences and some from other people who've shared their tales with me. It is also written from things that are currently happening at my place of employment, so I guess it is like a little journal also. So today or let me say since this is Sunday. It was Friday at work, and I was sailing along OK, and nothing much was happening a few calls here and there I was thinking about getting off work and jumping into the pool. Well it happened all hell broke loose, and every order that I had place on Thursday went down the tubes real fast. Everything was on the stupidity of the company; I cannot blame any one person. It was the same story that has been repeated a hundred times a day. It was the same reason and or excuse why they can't release a product or why they can't find the document, so on and so on. So here I am wasting another whole day just to fix the problems within my own company. One of the orders that was held was a client of mine that had an open account with us, for an estimated 150,000 dollars. And they held up the shipping of the order because they were 90 days past due on 15,000 dollars. By the history of this and most huge corporations, they are always late in paying. It is the corporate way; even my own company does it like that! So they (the Credit department) told me that I would have to get new credit applications and letters stating that this client of mine knows that they are on a net 30 terms with our company. Like they do not know this or something, God I hate stupidity, these people do have it rough. I am talking about the credit department. This is how they play god, they mess with your best clients and make it rough, and so I do what was needed. I lied to them, first after they told me what they wanted from the client I told them JUST WHAT THEY WANTED TO HEAR, I said it would be no problem, and I left and went back to my little box or cubical. I waited about three hours and then I went back to the same lady who by this time had forgotten everything we talked about. So she pulled up the account again and this time she looked at it and asked different question as to what was up. I told her that it had been taken care of and they would receive their money. Now the funny thing about this is it is the same person that loves to play this god person or position. However if she really knew what was happening, two things would happen, one she would not have released the order and made me give her the documents or two she should have collected the documents herself. Either way if she was the person she was trying to portray she would have asked the same questions over again. But I knew that in a few hours she would totally forget everything.

I get so tired of this, people trying to validate their jobs so they can have a job to validate. I do understand the reason why this happens. In every company the upper management watches to see who is working and who is not. If you make your job too easy, it seems like you are not working and then they question you as to what you do all day. So by their reasoning if you are stressed out and pissed off all day, they think you are working. All I hear all day is, YOU SHOULD BE ORGANIZED, that way things go smoother. However if things are smooth then they add more things to your plate. It is better to look busy than to really do the work.

Here is something else that I do and this scares the hell out of them, first I get pissed at the computer, NOTE: never get pissed at a person! During the time I am yelling or swearing at the computer, I say, WHERE IS MY UZI or something to the fact of I AM GOING POSTAL. Everyone around you looks and thinks that maybe this guy will shoot someone some day. This does a few things for me, first it allows me to do things my way, and two it makes them think twice about firing me. Who wants to be the one that fires someone if you think they are going to blast the place apart? No one wants to be the one that opens that box. So they always ask how things are going? I say they are just fine!

It is funny that everyone runs around touting stuff like, OPENNESS, and TRUTHFULNESS, GOOD WORK, HONESTY, ETC. and the first thing they break is all the stuff they tout. I have never seen so much back stabbing and double edged swords in a company in my life.

IN THE MEN'S ROOM

Now here is the place for real things that happen. I must pass along my apologies to the ladies of the corporate work force. Since I am not into being charged with sexual misconduct, there will be little to say on the women's behalf, in this subject matter. Or what happens behind closed doors in the area of the restroom. This is the domain of the male species, he is in control here, he will allow others of his kind to roam about but they must not mark their territory in the same place as you are marking yours. You must not look at the other male next to you. You may talk or look at the ceiling but do not make eye contact until the marking is done. These are some of the rules which are unwritten but yet followed very closely. You may talk to the person in the other stall, but it must be a general acknowledgement of the other person. If you know the other person you can make light of other subject matter or even make it a serious matter. But you cannot get into the meat of the matter until the duty is done and it is washed away. You step out of the hole in which you have released the burden you were carrying. The door opens you see the other person and the conversation continues, this time with more conviction. I want to take a moment and express one of my biggest concerns and try to figure out why men do this, not all men just some. And I know for a fact, women will be cheering me on. I know if this bugs me, it must rip the hell out of the female species. How do I say this? "FLUSH THE DAM TOILET WHEN YOU ARE DONE!" I can never figure this out. You are standing there, doing your thing, or sitting there doing it. You finish and then you look, everyone does. PUSH THE BUTTON, PULL THE HANDLE, what is it with this? Is it to prove that you can mark in a different color or shape? Is it you want others to know you can fill the air with your grace? Or is it you have never been potty trained properly to understand the intricate workings of a flushable toilet? This is disgusting; I can understand a broken toilet, or a second time around thing. But a deliberate no touch flush means that you are a SLOB!

Everything else is cool, missing the trashcan when you pretend you are Michael Jordan, splashing water all over when you splash your face. Standing looking in the mirror to make sure you are the best looking male species on the floor. Even letting one rip while washing up. This is a male thing and it is a moment of pride. This is called tooting your horn, announcing your presence in the male world. Making sure that the lesser males be warned. There has been a few times, and yes I am as guilty as the rest. You walk in; let one go, to make sure that others in the restroom know you are there. If there is a male already making his mark, he will respond if he thinks he is better. Your ears perk up at this response. So you strut over to an open stall check to see if the last ASSHOLE FLUSHED. Give a chuckle at the paper seats that are there for the prissy ones. Them dam things are a pain in the ass. They get stuck on your butt, and then they do not FLUSH, you have to check to make sure you did not stuff it in your pants after you are done. With that thing hanging out, you are finished if you have to confront a serious horn blower a few minutes later. So you find your position, you clear your throat or cough to let the other bucks know you are ready for rutting season! It is quite enough when it starts and it has to be done by accident or when something else makes a noise that is loader. Such as the toilet paper roll being used in another stall. Your opportunity is there, so you take your shot. You let a little ripper out. BRRRRR, the guy in the stall next to you knows he can do better. He lets one go. All of a sudden a third is heard in the stall in the corner. Now there are three. Now you are on the spot. Your next better be good or you are out of the running. You let it fly! Bam, You make sure you lift a little so you can use the echo of the bowl to enhance the sound. All of a sudden another blast comes from the other side of the restroom. Now there is four males competing for control of the restroom. The door is heard opening and everyone goes quiet, we do not want to give the competition any fore warning or the match that is in progress. You listen; the sound of his feet on the floor indicates what this intruder is there for. He is a quick marker, so you know he will be gone in a flash. The sound of a FLUSHING urinal is heard. A buck waiting to get on with the match turns a page, the sound of the page tells the quick marker to get out and let us finish. Well maybe I am taking things to extremes but it's funny when you think about it.

The restroom is a good place to do some quick venting, and no I do not mean bodily type. I mean when work is getting to you, you take a break and hope you run into a person you can rely on not to tell everyone, about what kind of day you are having. The restroom is a good area that the bosses do not enter or they have their own place of rutting. Let's face it the restroom is the last bastion of solitude in the work place. Everywhere you go, there are cameras and taped phone conversations and people watching your every move, accept in the restroom. Or at least for now anyway, I am sure they will find a way to make it legal to put a camera in the shitter so they can listen to you take a dump. I am sure once that happens; we will see a new show, the funniest toilet humor. Or some kind of laws being passed and people screaming and hollering about their rights and how they are being violated. The restroom is the only place a man can be a man and a woman can be a woman. You can let your hair down or scratch yourself without someone taking it the wrong way. You splash a little water on the face and look into the mirror to make sure you are still alive. Just in case the company told you were alive but they were only using the TELL'EM ANYTHING story to make you think you are alive. When in reality you are dead and they are using your body for some evil experiment in cyber workers and they have replaced your brain with a chip made in the corporate labs.

Think about it, you walk into work and you are on a little bit of a high, for what ever reason, traffic was good or you had a good breakfast, anything really. You reach into your pocket and pull out the card; it has a barcode on the back. You swipe it through a little gray box and the door opens. There is a sign overhead that states: PLEASE STORE PERSONAL BRAINS HERE. INSTALL COMPANY BRAIN AND PROCEED TO WORK STATION. So you follow the instruction, and head for your workstation. However before you start, you need the restroom fix to kick-start yourself. The door to the restroom opens, in your mind it sounds like the doors on the Enterprise from STAR TREK, whoosh the door opens, and you feel the corporate brain disconnect and your real brain reconnect. However as soon as you exit, your other brain is lost and the corporate brain is there waiting for you, and it asks: DAVE WHAT ARE YOU DONG DAVE? You tell HAL to shut up and get to work. It is something like that; look at the people that come into the restroom! They have this lost look on their faces and once in the restroom that same face changes to a human face. It is scary I tell you; to see someone you know make such a drastic change in seconds is weird. The procedures are the same no matter which restroom you enter. You walk in and take in the cool air; you make a quick scan of the area, looking for an open stall or urinal. You find one and enter, while shutting the door; a smile grows on your face. Now you are ready to drop your trousers and moon the company in a private way. No one can see you, however they can hear you, so you better not laugh or they will take you away. A man by himself in the bathroom stall, and laughing, he better have a good joke book in there.

Now I hate to bring this up, but I needed to say something about this, it has little to do with the restroom but it also seemed the best place to put this. We were in a training class, which was a good one this time. Everyone was doing good, time was flying by, which means the training instructor and the class was fun. After the class everyone piled out of the room as we always do, and piled into the elevator to go back up to the cubicles in which we live most of our lives. As we stood waiting for the elevator to open its doors to allow us into its' domain. I thought I should hit the can before I go back to work. The thought changed as the doors to the elevator opened. So I did the elevator shuffle, and it takes practice to do it right. You can tell the true elevator riders. They have this little wobble walk that resembles a penguin's walk more than anything. So we waddle in facing the back of the elevator and stop when we cannot waddle anymore. At this time we turn into little toys that shuffle the feet so you can turn around and face the door. Now the capacity of the elevator is 15, and I tell you we max that puppy out every chance we get.

Ok, we are all settled in, it is like a choreographed dance, enter, turn look at the person closet to the buttons. The button is pushed and everyone looks up at the numbers. The elevator is slow but smooth; reach our floor, which is on the tenth floor. It stops and begins to hum and hums and hums, a winy noise starts coming out of the ceiling, a banging and then a slapping noise. So we are packed in like sardines and this death trap decides to catch a few mice. My buddy grabs the doors and tries to open them, to no avail. The women start, I should have gone to the restroom before getting on this thing. I thought to myself, GREAT WHAT A THING TO SAY AT A TIME LIKE THIS. All of a sudden my balls start to fill and my bladder wants to burst. Now all I can think about is getting to the bathroom for a little bit of relief. After about ten minutes or so the elevator starts to slip, oh I forgot, we could hear other people on the other side of the door, laughing and cutting up at our expense.

So as the elevator starts to slide down the shaft of hell, everyone holds their breath, it was a literal inhale by all. We slid nine floors to the first floor where the doors opened and we had to climb the nine floors back to the top, AFTER we all went to the bathroom.

LUNCH

This is the time in the middle of the workday that people let their hair down just enough to blow steam at all the idiocies that go on inside the building. However you must be careful to whom you let the steam fly. Others among your co-workers will laugh along with you or sympathize with your plight. So you pour your heart out to them, just so they can use it against you when they can climb the ladder while using you as a rung to step on.

I must make this clear, your co-workers will not do this intentionally, and they do not mean you any real harm. But they will spill their guts to protect their own jobs. They will not go running to the boss man and ruin their position in the work place. They do not want to be outcasts among their friends. A person that does so is soon alienated in the work force and even looked down on from the higher ups. They will use this person to get what they want without promotion and or any awards at all. After they are finished with him or her they will exile them to the place from which they came. Which after a few months they will quit because of the cruelty imposed on them from their own co-workers for being a snitch. If you really want to know how a company operates and how well they treat their employees, spend a day or two in the lunchroom. The world of that company will be at your feet. Things you will find out, are who is the best worker, who is the best manager, who is hated and what policies are the stupidest. Where the company is going and how well it is doing in the market. You can find out what department is doing the worst or is the worst to work for, you can find out how much someone is making or not making. Who is dedicated to the company and who isn't?

When you are within the walls of the corporate structure, the control and the rules of the corporation apply. But when you are within the lunchroom and away from thinking about corporate rules and policies. The barriers are lifted to open the relief valve just enough to allow some of the pent up steam and anger to be vented. Most high officials avoid this place like the plague, they are not wanted in this domain, when they are there the entire atmosphere is changed and the rules of the corporation applies. It is quiet and everyone feels obligated to perform at lunch the way they have to at work. It is a place of relaxation so the workers can regenerate their energies. It is fascinating at the wealth of information you can find out about people and the lunchroom gossip. The stories and tales that are told and spun, all in the name of amusement and release for the enjoyment and pleasure of the employees who work within the walls of the corporation. A few years ago one of the funniest things happened in the lunchroom. It was the factory and everyone that eats in this lunch facility was considered the animals of the company. We played the part well, we yelled and talked on a lower male form of communication. The office workers would not come to this area of the factory, especially the women employees. However the women animals were welcome and joined in the festivities right along with the rest of the male sub-humanoids. It was the only way that we could handle the situation that we were in. dehumanizing work, it was good pay, but is sucked. To this day I do not know how many of the workers at that place handled it. It drove me to drugs and into a rehab center, well our little town did not have one of those and the company did not know how to handle the addiction problems that were coming to the company. I was the first, what an honor to bestow onto a company that had no idea I was coming and behind me were many more. But like corporate policy, deny everything and hope it will go away. Well I did go away, and the problem was still there. They knew what to do with the alcoholics of the factory, however the drugs that came to the plant were something else.

Anyway I am getting off track here. So there I was working my ass off and going to lunch to complain about how the work sucks. I was not alone in this matter, many of the workers, almost ninety-five percent of the factory work force was bitching about one thing or another.

The shift that I worked on was the graveyard shift and it was the worst. No life to speak of no friends but the ones you worked with. No sunshine, you had to put black plastic over your windows in the bedroom just so you could sleep. It was hard, you had to learn to eat breakfast at nine at night and dinner at seven in the morning. The only good thing is that the town allowed one bar to open at 6 in the morning to service the graveyard workers. It was an interesting place. Imagine getting ripped at eight in the morning. I tell you right now, even telling people that you worked the graveyard shift, they still did not understand you being smashed at eight in the morning. So the crew began getting a reputation of being a bunch of drunks. People do not understand something that is different, even though there is a perfect explanation. If I was smashed at eight at night and the same person came up to me, they would say "GO HOME AND SLEEP IT OFF" but being smashed at eight in the morning the response was "YOU DRUNK GET AWAY FROM ME" or if it was a friend it was "DON'T DO THIS TO YOURSELF" so you began to find other things to do, drink at home so you could still have your booze and no one would hassle you about it. Now this led to something that I nor anyone else in the factory ever expected to happened. It was a normal lunch hour and the gang was all there. We were covered in cast iron dust and grease, the usual dirt and grim that is a part of the everyday work at the plant. So I am sitting there eating my sandwich that I had brought to work in the typical black lunch box with the thermos of coffee or soda depending on the day.

The game to play is "EUCHRE" it is without a doubt an east coast game and even more a north east coast card game. It is a fast game and the betting ranged from coin to dollars even a friendly game to see how many you can play in an hour. Just to let you know how fast a four-member card game can be, the best in the plant played thirty-two games in an hour. That is how fast the hands are played. Everyone in the place had a deck of cards and everyone played. At work or at play in the bar anywhere, it was fun. So there I sit playing euchre with the buds at work, the conversation was the typical one, how is the machine running, how many pieces did you knock out today. Did you play your tickets today? Playing tickets is using the corporate system against itself so you can rack up many more pieces and make more money on piecework. These guys and myself thought we were getting away with something and getting over on the company, but we weren't. The company knew what was going on. And let us do it, they got the production they wanted and at a price which was less than we thought. Who knew? Then there was a lull in the conversation and the cards could be heard hitting the table where the fast card games being played. No time to talk at those tables, to much at stake. Out of my mouth came something that I would never admit to even on the rack. But it came nonetheless, I asked my partner across the table if he knew "WHAT SUSAN WAS UP TO ON GENERAL HOSPITAL"! The room went silent, the card games stopped and everyone turned and looked at me. Oh shit I knew I was a goner in the room full of animals. Then my partner looked at me and said, "SHE IS RUNNING AWAY WITH RYAN OR SOMETHING LIKE THAT" the room burst out in serious laughter. Everyone in the room was watching soap operas at home after work. We all knew the characters and who was doing what to whom; it turned into a chicken house of cackling hens. I could not believe it, for over a year I was keeping this dark secret that no one knew was going on and here everyone was doing the same thing and was afraid to say anything for fear of being ridiculed by their co-workers. For the rest of the hour and other hours during lunch we played euchre and talked about what was going on in the world of the soap operas.

During lunch break good things happen also. It is where the employees get together and talk about what has happened so far during the day. Ideas are exchanged and put into place when the workers get back to the job at hand. I see this all the time, the new employees ask the older ones how to do something to make the work go faster or seem less boring. Everyone is more than happy to help, it is like the mentor and the apprentice.

Lunchtime is one of the most neglected periods in a workday; most companies see it as time they have to pay for or time they cannot control. When in reality it becomes a free forum for discussion on the day's events. It is a place that the employees use to recharge the batteries for the next round of work obstacles. I see a lot of companies totally forget this area of the workday. Think about this, it is one ninth of the day. Or if it is a paid lunch, which is a half hour, that is one eighth of the workday. That is a lot of time going to waste. Everyone says that it is their own time and they can do anything they want. Well that is true, however what do you do at lunch? You talk about work, and no company is focused on using that time to teach or train or make the employee a part of the company. Here is an example; this is where the suggestion box should be! When someone is working they do not have time to write down the ideas in their head. It can be used to run training tapes if someone wants to watch it, maybe a new product is out and they want to get up to speed on it. What better way than to have a tape deck, so they can pop it in and get trained while on lunch.

All I hear is time management, but every time they try to change something it is the same thing they changed last time.

Ninety percent of the time, I am at lunch with my co-workers we talk about work and how we hate it or how stupid the company is. This to me is a total waste of time on the company's part and on the part of the employees. This time can be constructive and be used to help in bridging the gap between corporation and employee. More ideas are born and die in this one area than any other place in the plant or company. The reason is it is a free zone, and with a free zone comes freethinking. This area breeds, one of two things, it breeds discontent or it breeds loyalty. If the higher ups or executives' think it does neither, they are in for a rude awakening. Unions started in the lunchrooms. I have nothing against unions, just to say they are powerful groups in which corporations have to contend with. And they started in the lunchrooms. The corporations nowadays are so focused on what they think is right they are blinded to areas that can put them miles ahead in the work place, just by opening their eyes. Employees know this and see it everyday. It is because they are in the trenches and doing it. They know what will work and what will not. Again that is why unions got started, the people got tired of bullshit and not getting anything for it. It will happen again, and the corporation will fight it and history will repeat itself, just because the companies refuse to think that people are an important part of organization. Computers are the wave of the future, and companies think that they can replace people by using things such as the Internet. They will soon find out, you still need the human touch and that human touch will be harder and harder to control because of the years of alienation that was bestowed on the worker in the past. Nothing I say here will change anybodies mind. However mark my words it will come to pass. The saying, "IF YOU DO NOT LEARN FROM THE PAST YOU ARE DOOMED TO REPEAT IT" is a true statement and has been proven time and time again. We are truly idiots when it comes to learning things. We as a species can send a man to the moon but cannot figure out how to work together.

PAYDAY

Now here is the day that everyone waits on. It is the most popular day and the most scrutinized day of any within the work month.

This is the day of rejoice. It is the day when there is an underlying happiness within the workplace. Until the checks get opened, then the truth hits. It comes in statements like, "I PUT ALL THAT EXTRA TIME IN FOR THIS"! Or "THIS WON'T COVER MOST OF THE BILLS", etc. very seldom is it a happy time after opening the checks. It is a perceived disappointment; the numbers do not match what the workers think they are worth. However when the higher ups open their checks or statements of pay, they do one of two things. Either they smile and are happy at what they see or they act just like the workers, and think they are not being paid what they are worth.

This is where money management comes in, I think and have made suggestions to companies about teaching or holding classes on money management to teach employees on how to handle money. And not those stupid classes where they bring a broker in and tell you what to invest in. I am as guilty as the next person is, when it comes to spending money foolishly. Let's face it, no one ever taught me how to handle the dollar. Hell they never taught me the meaning of the dollar. Me, it was, give me the check, let me cash it and where is the bar! Then for the next two weeks it was borrowing money from everyone to survive the week. I did not know how to handle money. My dad always called it "BURNING A HOLE IN MY POCKET" it is also the reason why the lotteries setup payments for the winners. We as a working class were taught and we believe that having a lot of money is something we were not allowed to have. So we self-destruct our good fortune because we believed we did not deserve it. Well I for one have learned that I am worth it and, damn it, I deserve it also. It is the attitude that I have when I apply for a job, I am worth this much or more, and if you Mr. Corporation don't see that I am worth it, then we part ways. I will not settle for anything less than what I am worth. Why should I? Who says I am worth this much or that much. I know what I can do, and I know what I can do for the corporation. If they think that I am not worth it, it is their loss not mine.

It is our own self-esteem that will determine the amount of money that we will make. I attended a sales motivational seminar: the speaker was very good and knew a lot about sales and the attitudes of clients as well as sale people. He talked a lot about making the deal and reading people whether it was on the phone or in person. He also made a statement that at first I could not believe. Then after checking into it I had discovered that it is true. More than three quarters of the world had negotiations in their everyday dealings. What I mean by this is that you can go into a store and negotiate a price for the product you want to buy. This was an eye opening thought! He even told us that everything is negotiable. I could not believe that everything is negotiable, in the United States. Hell this man was English and I thought to myself that I knew more about the American economy than he did. What I came to find out was the economy had nothing to do with negotiations. With this thought running around in my head, the opportunity presented itself so that I in fact could test this theory of his. My car was in need of some brakes, and I knew it was going to cost so much. Well the sign outside the building said, brakes 59.95 per axle. However I needed to read closer at what the sign said. It read BRAKES 59.95 AND UP PER AXLE. This was interesting, which meant that the price was negotiable. All I knew is that the minimum was 59.95 per axle. It did not say who or why the price was set it just stated that it started there. So my question was, who gets the 59.95 price and why? Well they are a good company, and I still use them today, the reason is that the first time I went in to have the brakes checked, they said that it was a free inspection. I thought YEA RIGHT, however it was free and did not cost me a dime. Now I was back and needed the brakes done. They put the car on the rack and did the inspection. I also asked for an oil change too. It took them about twenty minutes to check the car out. The verdict was bad; I should have made them change the brakes the first time. Now the rotors were bad, they even showed them to me before they took them off. It was chewed up, I was pissed, I knew from experience that rotors were close to one hundred bucks and this was before labor. So the manager figured the price for the brakes both axles and oil change. Total was a incredible four hundred and fifty five dollars. Of course it was lifetime brakes, which still sucked for the price. I looked at the manager and he looked at me, I turned my head and looked at my car in pieces in the garage bay. That is how they get you also, they tell you how much it is and then let you look at your car in pieces on the floor. What are you going to do; your car is not running any more? However what I found out is that if you take your car into a shop and they check it out and find something wrong, they must give you the option of taking it to another mechanic which means they have to put the car back together again in the condition that it came in, you must remember that you drove it in, you should be able to drive it out. So I told him that I could not afford or have the money to pay such a price. The manager told me that he could not knock more than forty bucks off the price. I looked at him and told him this is the deal, I HAVE THREE HUNDRED AND TWENTY DOLLARS and that is it. Other wise put the car together and I will do it myself. So the manager sat at his desk and punched the calculator a few times. Of course he did not show me what he was figuring. After about ten minutes he looked at me and said that it would be tight but he could give the oil change to me for free and do the brakes for the three hundred and twenty dollars including tax. I said OK and they did a great job.

This showed me that everything is negotiable if you are willing to ask for it. We as Americans are being too easy on stores and corporations. They set the price and we buy it at that price. I ask you now, WHY? Who says that we have to pay so much for a car or even a loaf of bread? It used to be the price was set at what we could negotiate. Now it is whatever the company wants and how much they want to make off the product. The terminology is WHAT THE MARKET WILL BEAR, what this statement really means is what the public will pay. Not what the product is worth. If the public refuses to pay the price of something, then the company will drop the price until it finds what that product will sell for. You too can do this with your paycheck, and the money you ask for. However if you go into a fast food joint and demand five hundred a week to flip burgers. You will receive just what you asked for! A bag of nothing, and the reason is the same. The product you asked for could not bear the price you wanted. It is all negotiations, how many times have you gone into a job interview and they ask you what your price is for working there. Everyone or most everyone says it is negotiable, however when the interviewer says the job pays this much, you say ok! What the hell is that? They want to know if you are willing to negotiate the price. Look at it like this, if you are selling their product and you are working under the negotiation status, and you are not willing to negotiate for your self. How in the hell can you negotiate for the company?

This is your life you are discussing! Why would you want to put it in someone else's hands? They could give two shits about you and your dealings. Do you know how many times someone comes into their offices and tells them some wimpy story about how they are broke and have seven kids to feed. It is bullshit, they want someone that is willing to stand on their feet and command the situation. Male or female it does not matter, if you ask for a price and they tell you that the position only pays so much, and the pay is what you are looking for, say ok. They will not kick you out of the office for trying to get more money! They will even give you the respect of a human being. It comes down to this, NO ONE WILL WATCH OUT FOR YOU, the only people that come close is family. Friends might sometimes but when the shit hits the fan, take a look around, you will be alone, unless you pay someone to stand by you. Then they will as long as the money lasts. Example: OJ, need I say more, where are all his fancy lawyers now? His money is gone and so are they.

You cannot count on the lottery either, sure play it if you want however don't build your hopes and dreams on winning. I will make a bet with you, I bet I will become a millionaire before you win the lottery!

SUPPLY AND DEMAND

This is one of the hardest things that a company can keep up with. It is never ending and on going. It never gives anyone a break or takes a day off. It never allows a moments rest with the employees or the corporate executives. It is the true monkey on your back.

This has to be one of the most unforgiving positions within any corporations. You have the company screaming at you to keep cost down. Then you have sales people screaming at you that there are not enough products to sell in a reasonable fashion.

It is one of the greatest balancing acts that I have ever seen. And I tell you I have never seen it performed very well, even by some of the best buyers.

You are probably wondering why I have chosen this chapter as a subject matter for a book called "TELL'EM ANYTHING"? Well it is simple, in this area of any corporation you have the highest use of telling them anything, just to get them out of your hair. And I mean both Higher-ups and lower class employees. Everyone wants a piece of your ass, in this department, and no one is ever happy with the outcome.

I cannot for the life of me understand why anyone would want to put up with the bull shit that goes on in this department. However because of the situation that these people are in, they end up with some of the best tell'em anything stories ever. They do have to be creative in the way the tales are told and delivered. Not only do they have to lie, but they have to do it with such flare that you must accept their reason at face value.

The life of a buyer begins in the trenches and he or she digs himself or herself deeper. However one of the good things about being a buyer for a company is that you are relatively safe in a position not many want. Some of the other good things are the perks that you receive from the vendors and sales people that you do business with. They all try and get you free stuff, just to make you happy. It is a give and take situation, they give and you take.

Here is a tale of a purchaser that tried to TELL'EM ANYTHING in a big way. I found this out the hard way, well sort of by accident. I was doing the computer-selling thing, and this particular company had a bad habit of not keeping product in stock so we can sell it. They were always worried about too much product on the floor that could not be moved. Then the price would drop and they would lose profit. This is where the purchasing person comes in. However this company would not hire or train the buyers properly and because of this they would never order the right amount of stock to cover even the orders that were being placed. We were selling the product and they were not ordering it. We ended up loosing orders to other companies that were doing it right. However this company was so blind to what was going on that they did not want to admit to the fact that, their purchasing department did not have a clue to what was needed to increase the sales. So anyway, I had this regular client and they would buy 30 systems a month, it was not a big order considering some of the other orders on the books. But it was a good amount of product. They would not consider this or any other accounts orders in need of the product. They would look at how much they had to buy with and order just enough for the big accounts and let all the others slip by or make them wait.

They would place an order with the manufacturer and then delay the order time and time again. You would look at the computer screen and find the date that the purchasing person entered as the date of product arrival. Come to find out, this date was not a real date of arrival. It was a date of hope of arrival. They would call the manufacturer and the manufacturer would tell them what date the product would ship. The purchasing person would then say I would like it on such and such a date. But they did not listen to the manufacturer. They just said I want it at this time.

Well every time we the salesperson would tell our clients that the product would be in on this date. They would change the date of arrival, and the only way we would know is to check the date the next day. They would change the dates that often. There was no way to tell or even guess when the product would arrive. They would do this day in and day out.

Well one day I had an order and the purchaser and the person placing the order did not set the product off to the side. I looked up the products in the computer system and it told me that they were available and ready for sale. So I placed the orders, man did all hell break loose over that. They told me that I could not have the product because it was allocated to another client. I argued, then why were those systems not placed on a priority status and that way they would have never shown up in the system. I got the order and shipped them. But from then on they gave me a rash of shit and got real nit picky on everything I did. Well it was my fault, I followed their rules and they did not follow their own standards. For me being right and a low life salesperson, they just made it hard for me to get product. So this went on for months, and since I was right I was not going to back down to their petty jealousies. This company was full of scared people who had no idea that they could be doing a good job instead of being TELLING THEM ANYTHING type people. They worked harder at making sure that the higher ups knew they were working, instead of working and doing their job. It was crazy, here all I heard was sell, sell, sell, and they did nothing but make it hard to sell.

They the company would put out catalogs with specials and not have the product in stock. They would then tell us to up sell them or cross sell them. This was a tough position to put sales people, who had enough troubles in prospecting clients. After the fiasco with the products has subsided, I was browsing the system and ran across an obscure skew number. It looked sort of familiar but was entered in a weird way. With further investigation I found out it was product that most of the sales floor was waiting on. The date that this product was to hit the floor was almost four weeks before the scheduled time. What they did in the system was create a new product number and route all the systems to that skew number. This way no one on the floor but a privileged few would know the systems came in, and they could sell them to their clients at their leisure. Well I checked and called all the manufactures before I brought this to the attention of my manager. I found out they even added a letter to the ID number; I cannot believe what these people will do just to protect their jobs. Or make them selves look better than the rest of the floor. Now what is really amazing is these are the same middle management that conducts the teamwork sales classes. They continue to tell everyone to work together and be a part of the team. But these rules do not apply to them, which with the mind set in that place of business is par for the course. Now here is the funny part of this fiasco. If these middle management personnel were smart, they would have floored the product and not told or entered them into the system, however if they did that the higher ups would have asked why are these systems not available to the floor or they would have asked to see the PO's which they did not have. So that means they did not have them sold, but were planning on it in the future. Who knows, it is so hard to have faith in a company who says one thing and forces you to follow the rules while the very person that set the rules stabs you in the back and yells at you when you cannot make the numbers.

There are a few people I am sad for, one is my manager, he is a hard working person and he is smart in the books and the way things should work. However he is not to wise in the ways of the world, he thinks the world of corporations will follow it's rules in which they have set up. When I brought the problem to his attention, he chewed my butt off. The reason is he said they were saved for this other company, and if I placed an order against them, there would be hell to pay. I said fine, and by the end of the day the word got out about the systems and there was a battle of the managers over the systems. They released the systems to the floor for everyone to sell. Which in the end means I was right in the first place.

So not only can you TELL'EM ANYTHING you can WRITE'EM ANYTHING too. The lies that permeate the corporate structure is wondrous. How can a company continue dealing in lies and make a profit? It is easy, TELL'EM ANYTHING Keep them fighting among themselves. The company will go on and the information that is used against the employees or for the employees will be up to the executives of that corporation.

My co-workers call me the conspiracy theorist; I am always looking for the reason that a company is doing something. I hate to say it but some of my co-workers are new to the industry and fresh out of college. They have not lived in the real world of corporate law. They think that in a corporate battle the rules are set, and there are no spies or lying or cheating or backstabbing. They think it is an even playing field, and I cannot tell them any different. It is like a child who you have told time and time again not to touch the fire! They think you are crazy, until they get burned they do not understand what they are up against. If you want to climb the corporate ladder, you better get use to it. You have two choices in corporate life. Be content where you are or fight for your right to climb the ladder. There is a trick that you can use to dig yourself into the trenches of a corporation that makes it very difficult for them to root you out. If you are the target of attack from the management department, which sees you as a threat, you will be well prepared for battle. The first rule of thumb, never let them see you coming, stealth is the best method. I do not mean be sneaky or underhanded, I mean do not let them know who you are. If you want to climb the ladder within a corporation, you must first become apart of the corporation. The people you start with are people you never knew until you were hired. So why should these people whom you have known for four months hold you back from climbing out of the trenches? They are just like everyone else, very nice and helpful but unwilling to make their mark in life. They will unconsciously try to keep you in the trench because it makes them feel better. It is not because they care about you, they do not want to look like the unmotivated person they are.

THE GET AWAY

How far will you go? When it comes to getting away with something at work? Think about this one, many people even the most honest will try to get away with something. It is human nature; you take the extra long break or pick up that pen or even a roll of toilet tissue.

Getting away with something at work is like being on a safari the big game hunt. You beat yourself both mind and body to achieve the goal of the big kill. However at work that goal or kill might be as insignificant as a bad excuse for being late.

Living in the world of corporate America many things happen that change the views you once held in life. Stress is one of the main reasons for problems within the work place. The more stress and pressure that is applied the more problems arise.

Let's take a look at a co-worker of mine. We have been trying to increase the sales volume for months. Everyday the managers and higher ups turn up the pressure to get the results out of us and everyone else. However it seemed that the more pressure they would apply the lazier this guy and others would get. They would find many projects to keep them from doing the intended work that was requested. This goes back to the defiant teenager. Remember when you were a teenager or if you have teens of your own. No matter how much you were screamed at or how much you scream, the deafer you got and the deafer your teens became. No one likes to be barked at, you don't like it, so why would you think that the people that work for you would like it? What just because you paid them a wage or salary, this gives you the right to bully someone? I don't think so, and time and time again the employees will prove that your barking will do more for your vocal cords that anything else in the company.

Oh don't get me wrong; if you spare the rod you spoil the employee. I can see it now everyone that read the last statement is nodding their heads. Well you that are nodding must realize, that you are the child and if the company did not scream you would do nothing to promote or progress the profits of the company, in which they are paying you a check to do that very thing. Yes this is a mild catch twenty-two, people are lazy at heart and if you let them be lazy then they will be lazy. However they also want a sense of belonging, and will do good work to be apart of something. You as a manager must harness this power within your people and make it work for both you and them.

Go too far on the pendulum and they will steel you blind or not work for you. Swing it too far the other way; they will do the same thing. Too much pressure or not enough will have the same results. This is a tough balancing act that the manager and the company must do just to complete the tasks at hand. If you do not know what you are doing the employees will sense this and they will start looking for things TO GET AWAY WITH. The most frequent form of getting away with something is what I call TIME STEELING. This is a tough one to control and it is the easiest to get away with. You must learn the art of steeling time. First rule, you must look as if you are not steeling time. You might ask why make it look like you're not steeling time when you are steeling time? The answer to that question is, it is a game. If you play it as a game then you will understand the rules. If you play for keeps you will loose. You must learn that the company holds all the cards and will only tolerate so much game playing. However if you play it right, you can keep the dealer busy while you steel your time. Now that I have totally confused you again we shall see what time there is to steel. Never or barely touch clock in or out time, this area of time is way too easy to track and you will loose the game fast. Restrooms are the best time Steelers and there is nothing the company can really do about it. They might yell and scream, but they cannot deny you restroom privileges. So you can even push this area to the extremes. If they fire you for too many restroom breaks you can take them to court and sue them. So they will have to find new reasons as to why they are letting you go.

It is interesting that I was writing this chapter, at work today the company did one of the biggest chicken shit things a company could ever do. They had a mass firing or lay off. Well it can't be a layoff, because they were hiring people the same day. This sent shock waves throughout the company. Just five days ago, they canned about a third of the management team.

You can tell it was politically motivated, because the managers that were fired some of them were good people, and damn good managers.

Come to find out that the new president is firing anyone that could be a threat to his position. Check this out, here is the letter he emailed to everyone in the company after he did the slash and burn today.

Fellow Employees,

As I stated in my letter to everyone back on the 24th of July, it is critical that we reduce expenses in order to improve profitability. With this in mind, we took a major step forward today in our effort to build our company into the powerhouse it will soon become, by adjusting the size of our team. While it is never easy to say good-bye to friends and colleagues, sometimes it is a critical element that is needed to insure that the rest of the organization flourishes. I know you all join me in wishing all of these people the best success in whatever direction their careers take them.

In that same letter I talked about the importance of sales and customer service to our organization, since without customers who honor us with their purchases, we have no value or purpose. In order to give our valuable salespeople the best possible chance of selling more, we have reorganized certain support functions so that they can be better equipped to meet the challenges of today's marketplace. Critical elements of this plan include the fact that it is based on trust and giving people more direct control over their areas of responsibility as well as the accountability that goes along with this. I also told everyone how important I felt training was to our company. Our new structure has been designed to provide everyone with meaningful growth opportunities.

Change is never easy; in fact, it is very uncomfortable. However, I know that you will all agree that most things in life that are good, require at least some level of discomfort before the good part kicks in. in the weeks ahead, I am sure we will all feel some anxiety too long before we will all experience the improvement in our results that we are all looking for. If you have any questions, feel free to contact me directly.

For now I am going to ask each of you to help by doing more than you used to do. You are still with us because we believer that you are the people with the most skill, drive and desire and that you will all do whatever is needed to maximize our results. We can make great things happen by working together. Let's do it!

This letter was written two hours after he terminated sixty people from the building. The way they did it was really chicken shit, you would walk into the company and the banner was flying the first of the month. Everyone felt a little pride, and then two days later it hit. You walked into the lobby and there was an army of security guards there. The rule of this game was, if your ID badge did not scan, you were fired. The guard would escort you to your desk and get your things and out your went. It scared the living shit out of everyone in the building.

The letter in my opinion was in the same style of Brutus's speech after he just murdered Cesar. Granted he the new president had to write something, but to say by trashing the lives of sixty people without warning and saying it is a good thing. Is both arrogant and mean. The good thing that comes out of things of this nature is that in time the truth does come out. Such as the IRS was wandering the halls of the company without the knowledge of the company. Which is why the corporate executives were very upset. How in the heck did they get past security? And it makes you wonder if the salaries of the beheaded employees were done to payoff the IRS. I do not know about the facts behind it but the rumor mill works overtime when sixty heads lay rioting on the doorsteps of a place that calls itself paradise.

The company did nothing but dangle carrots in everybody's faces and sat back to see what happened. I was sad for the VP he was one of the most honest and nicest people to work with. He really did care, but he also knew how to get people involved with the company. This however was seen as a threat when the new president came in and the VP was the first to go. All the groundwork he did was laid to waste. It never had a chance to develop into the best organization around. It is the rule of thumb, NICE GUYS FINISH LAST. If you want to keep your job are you going to fight for it or just roll over and die? Yes I know there are jobs that you must do to get by, however what I am getting at is, if you and a co-worker are up for the same position, only one of you can have it. Who will it be, if both are equally qualified, then what do you do. The job will always go to the one that is most aggressive and or hungry. The other will always complain that it is not fair, because he deserved it more. That statement my friend is horse shit, if you want the job, then go get the job, other wise shut the hell up.

Nothing bugs me more than a sniveling person who thinks the world owes them something. If you want to work in the environment of sharks and you play the otter, your ass is going to be eaten. You must learn and adapt or be consumed by the sharks. I'm not saying that it is all bad, however you better be ready when the tough times come.

It's like the lady who found the rattlesnake on the road dying; she reached down and took it in her arms. She took the snake home and made a warm bed for it to rest. Everyday she fed it with an eyedropper and fixed its' broken bones. This went on for four months; the woman loved this snake and made sure that it was strong and ready to rejoin the world. She was so excited when that day came. The snake was excited also, the woman picked up the snake and took it outside to set it free. As she laid the snake down, it jumped up and bit her on the neck. It pumped its poison into the woman. The woman dropped the snake and screamed as she fell back onto the ground. As the woman lay there dying she looked over to the snake and asked WHY HAVE YOU DONE THIS? I took care of you and brought you back from death. The snake slithered up to her, looked her in the eye. MADAM I THANK YOU FOR YOUR HELP, BUT I AM A SNAKE, DID YOU EXPECT ANYTHING ELSE?. The snake slithered away as she died watching him.

She knew the snake was a snake, she knew his habits and what he was, so why did she get upset when the snake did just what a snake does? People can be the same way when it comes to corporations. They sit there and think that just because they do this or that for the company that the company will be different or treat them special than what they have done before. What everyone keeps missing is that the company will do just what it has always been doing. So don't act surprised when it does something you knew it would do.

Another interesting turn of events happens when a company slashes and burns the people in its organization, then turns around and writes a letter of how great the company will be with all the dead beats gone. It creates uneasiness within the ranks, rumors fly about who will be next on the chopping block. This tactic starts a rat-jumping situation whether the company wanted it or not. People start to quit and leave the company, and some are good people. Who wants to work under conditions in which you do not know if you will be next? They give guidelines in which to follow to keep your position, then after things settle they change the rules again and it starts all over again.

Now I must concede, some companies do well by their employees, and they also have to carry the burden of companies who screw people over. The new technology is turning corporations into the new sweatshops of the 21st century. Instead of shoes or clothes, it is phones and sales. They have the taskmaster who walks around yelling at everyone to do the job or they will be fired. These companies do carry a double standard in the way company rules and laws are written and followed.

I spent most of the day today, giving out my name and number to fellow employees. Everyone thinks they are going to be canned any day. Now what kind of happy horseshit is that? How can anyone expect to work under conditions of stress and ambiguity? These are good people and all they want is to feel safe and to be able to take care of their families. Look everyone knows there is no such thing as security anymore in the work force. However companies spend more money on retraining people than they do worrying about keeping the ones they have trained.

WORK PALS

There are the people you work with and people you associate with. Sometimes they are one in the same and then sometimes you will not even associate with them after hours.

Work pals are friends you come to know at the work place. They do come in all shapes and sizes. They dress differently and think differently some of them did not have a clue as to what the world is all about. Others think the world is all about them. I must make a statement here, PEOPLE WHO THINK THEY KNOW IT ALL, ANNOY US WHO REALLY DO. Yes I am one of those people who think that I know it all, however if I am proven wrong I will give credit where credit is due. Where do you want to start? Let's dog the people, who irritate me, there is the one guy at work that is a nice enough person in his own right. However he does have a habit of cutting others down to make himself look good. This person is a helpful and sort of considerate person. I know you know a person like this, they will tell at joke that is a funny one but uses a person in the group as the butt of the joke. Instead of generalizing he or she will point it out. This makes the person feel big inside but it is short lived. However the person that was the butt, will carry that tiny bit of meanness around for a long time.

To give an example: If you are fat, and you are swimming with your friends and this person comes a long and makes a statement like wow I can't believe the water level went up when you got in. Everyone has a chuckle, the person making the statements makes sure that everyone knows that he made it and everyone laughs. Even the one it was pointed at. But that person dies a little more inside. I use to be the one on the receiving end of these jokes. But now I make a point to say, WHY DO YOU HAVE TO CUT EVERYONE DOWN WHEN YOU MEET THEM? Their response is always the same IT WAS A JOKE! I would in turn tell him A JOKE IS SOMETHING THAT IS FUNNY, AND IT IS NOT A PUT DOWN TO A PERSON. Of course that person does not speak to you again unless he or she has to. It is best that way, no one needs that aggravation on top of all the stress work puts on you. You must learn to stand on your own two feet when it comes to people like this. I learned and I tell you my life is much better just because I speak what I think, I also consider what I am about to say also. You never burn a bridge until you know the bridge is burnable. One of the most important things that I have learned about the people you work with is you do not know them. Everyone is wearing a work face, and no one shares anything about their life outside of work until they get to know you. Work is a place that you can know someone but never really know them. You have to wear your armor if you want to make it over the first hurdles the company sets up. You do not have time to interact with the others; you must focus on work and its concerns. There will be plenty of time to socialize after you get settled in. Let's face it, you are not there to make friends, you have been hired to do a job. If you do not do that job you will be looking for another one very soon. Friends become your friends naturally. So let it happen naturally, they last longer and they can help you out later on and you can help them out too. A friend at work is a good thing; he or she can help with the stress thing, and give you a shoulder to cry on when things are not going so well. It also works the other way around too.

I must admit to you that I am a people watcher; I love going to the mall and watching people and the way they act. It is the same at work, when I have time of course.

I am not sure what it is, maybe charisma or just the fun of people. But I have a habit of attracting people. People just like being around me, and that is good, however sometimes they want to know everything about what I do? I have a flair for life and enjoying it. I think this is why I notice people more; I try not to shun them. They are people with feelings and emotions. There is this one lady at work, whom I don't know, she is extremely overweight, but a nice person. Yes I know, I am fat and I know the kiss of death for a fat person is YOU ARE SUCH A NICE PERSON, god I hate that. It is a battle that I must fight everyday. I cannot blame anyone but myself, no one put a gun to my head and said; EAT THAT CAKE OR I WILL SHOOT YOU! Well maybe I thought the cake said it. Anyway the fight goes on, so this woman at work would walk around and no one would talk to her, they would not look at her or even acknowledge that she existed. So I said hi, now I know what you are thinking. This woman was so starved for attention she took it the wrong way. Well I did notice in her eyes a sense of happiness, and she wanted more from those words of kindness. I did not push it and just talked to her, I would say good morning, and complement her on a hair change, or a new dress. She started to feel good about herself, and it showed in her work and the way she walked around. One of the hardest things to deal with in life is being fat. The doctors call it obesity, which is the politically correct word. But everyone knows you're fat. However everyone has this moral obligation to keep his or her mouths shut. It is mean to tell someone they are fat. It hurts their feelings, so what we do is the very thing that I have been writing about, TELL'EM ANYTHING, but the truth. It is sad that we do this in everything we do, listen I know it hurts when someone uses the fatty thing towards me. But it is the truth; the thing is there is a nice way to say it and a mean way to say it. You do not have to point at someone and say YOU ARE A FAT SLOB, as if we didn't know that! Oh wow, am I glad you pointed that out to me! I was wondering why the refrigerator was empty all the time. Oh and that is why my pants are tight, you think? But we are looked down on in the work place as well in the social arena. The reason why fat people are either very happy or very sad is because we have to compensate for un-acceptance in our social environment. I am a serious yoyo person, up one day and down the next. I deal with a lot of high corporate executives, who judge many of their consultants and business partners on looks rather than abilities. This is naturally normal, if a person can't keep his or hers weight in check how can they run my company. However everyone has their problems, some are more visible than others. But we are a society of looks and presumed appearances. It is all around us, in our advertising and media exposure. When in reality there are more not so pretty people than are good-looking ones. This too is a form of TELL'EM ANYTHING, our society tells us this is what we all should look like, and then bombards us day in and day out with offerings that does the exact opposite. We are losing the battle of who we are, and what we want. We fight day to day just to keep up with the bills because our society told us that we are to live this way. The stress that is put on us to achieve the small amount of reward for the effort that we have put in, translates into a DFC attitude. Now I know a lot of you are wondering what the HELL IS DFC? I use to wonder that myself. I was managing a theme park and the kids I would work with, wrote this on the walls or in the can. It was everywhere. I was just old enough to not know what it means. I am sure some of you have figured it out by now. It is three letters that have come to mean many things to me.

Here I was learning something from kids who looked at life differently than me. I found out it was not just one or two, but more than seventy percent of the youth that worked under me. We worked side by side, or that is how I saw it. I was the boss and they were the workers. I was a good boss and won many thanks from the youths under me. But they still wrote on the walls with DFC. One time it was scratched into the lens covers of one of the cameras. It was at this point that I had to find out what was happening and what DFC really meant. So I started to study and really take an interest in the kids that worked for me. First I found out that DFC means DON'T FUCKING CARE. I could not believe this, why were these kids writing this on the walls and everywhere else in the city? I was furious at them, however I did not say anything, because I knew they would not do things unless there was a reason. You might ask how I came to this conclusion? Well it was the lens cover, if they really did not care, they would have done it on the lens. But they knew that I would find out who did it and fire them. So they also knew that I was a fair manager and would do the right thing. What I discovered is these kids as I thought of them at first were young adults wanting to be responsible for their own lives. Here they were in charge of themselves while mom and dads worked or were gone. They took care of each other and found out that each other is the only people they could trust. Me I was part of the system and did not trust them. I gave them stupid rules to follow, and made them do things that they seemed ridiculous. Now on the defense, they did not know that I had to have things done a certain way, or it was my butt. I was a bitch dog manager and did not know it. I knew something had to be done. So I made the youths responsible for different things. Such as; the park had a serious theft problem. The registers were coming up short hundreds of dollars a week. This was at the time I was hired to fix the problem. I told the owners of the park that in my area the registers would stop coming up short within ten days. Well my assistant almost fell on the ground laughing at my statement. They had tried to straighten out the registers for months and could not get them right. So here comes this cocky man who no one knew, and making statements like this. The answer was simple; you had to make the people running the registers responsible for their actions. Once the kids were responsible for the cash, two things happened. First they realized that if they were the only ones on the register they would be the ones that would pay for the shortage. Second they started to look out for each other on how the money was handled. If I did not care why should they? The rules I made were for everyone, and no one even myself broke the rules. There was no double edge sword; it was the same for everyone. Plus you could not bend the rules either, once they knew you were flexible, the game was up, and they were back to the old ways.

The people you work with can make you or break you. They come in all shapes and sizes. Sure some people are a real pain, but that doesn't mean you have to be a pain back. You just do not deal with them, they are working PALS, and you do not have to take them home. You do not have to socialize with them, you have to work with them, and if you keep it like that your life will be much better. Now I am not saying that you will not run across that person that you connect with and have some good times with. Hell you could even meet your future spouse. What I am saying is people are different and you must realize this.

Just the other day, well as a matter of fact it was today. I was at work and it was a good day. People are stressed and worried because yesterday they told us that they (as in the company) will be looking at a couple of people and if they do not bring their numbers up they will be gone. Of course they failed to mention which two people. So as a result some of the team became very unnerved. They became panicked and talked about how the company is doing this or that. They took it personally; they talked about how they hated the job, and the things about it. Most of it was aimed at me, and the reason why is, they think I have an inside track as to who is going to get the ax. When in reality I had no clue. I had to worry about my own stuff because I could be one of the dead. And the reason for my death would not be because of poor work habits, it would be because of fear of me taking their position. I was a threat to them, and I was to a point. However I was asked to become a manager for the company and I turned them down twice already. The company still cannot understand my reason for this action. The reason is I am not willing to give my life to a company that was not willing to back the people that worked so hard for it. There was way too much back stabbing going on in the management pool. And the company would stir their little world every chance it got. They did not pay enough for me to jump into those waters. One of the things that I do like about working for companies is the variety of people that work there. There is this one guy at work, he is young and funny, now what is interesting about him is his out look on life. Let me set up the scenario, ok we are in cubicles the size of breadboxes, about six feet by four feet. And they wonder why people shoot each other in the work place. They stick you in the box, tell you how great it is, and then turn up the pressure. Well this co-worker who sits behind me, which is only three-foot aisle ways. We all talk on the phones doing sales, computer sales that is. I love computers and I do like sales, but a BOXED COMPUTER SALES PERSON is a little hard to handle. So you work side by side with all these people total of eight in an area made for two, but everyone has a wall. I say eight that are the ones that are connected to my BOX in someway. Now I am a very out going person. I have a voice that carries and people listen to every word I say. They do not say much about it, however. I do tell my clients that I am the greatest sales person in the world. Of course all my co-workers get a kick out of this. So this one day, I was having trouble with my system, and my PAL behind me, whom happens to be black, is a wiz kid when it comes to finding things for the MAC computers, he knows the codes and the SKU's. He asked me if he could sit in my chair. I got up and sat in his. Now I brought one of the office chairs in, my butt must be comfortable for me to work. So he is sitting there and I am sitting in his chair. Over walks another friend who was in training with me. We hit it off right away, so he walks over and him being a smart ass, he starts to talk to the black dude in my chair. Now mind you I am sitting like two feet away. So I fall into the rhythm of things.

I'll call this guy Bill, and the dude that walked up will be Ken. So Ken starts in on Bill as if he was me. Without a beat I started doing Bill. Now what happened next I will not forget for a long time. We're busting up with this routine, when Bill starts acting like me. Now what I am saying is he did a perfect imitation of me. My mannerisms my speech, he slouched in my chair and it was perfect posture at that. He even used my phrases that I use all the time. He started to talk about this book that I am writing and about the movies that I am working on. He started to spout things about conspiracy theory stuff. It took me back a step or two. I was shocked at how I sounded, and I was shocked at how much these people were paying attention to my actions and words. Ken and I were laughing our Asses off. Here was Bill, who is black and I am white, and he was doing a damn good impression of me, and it was funny as shit. He had us rolling on the floor. I am not sure if the impression of that moment is even coming across in this paragraph or not. I am still chuckling about it. To see yourself through the eyes of another is really interesting. He had it down, how I answered the phone and what I would say when something went wrong, or when I couldn't find something on my desk.

It was an eye opening experience. Now people can only do this if you trust them. Everyone around me was good people; some are stranger than others. But strange is only something you are not use to. If something is different then we as people seem to want to pick on it or make fun of it. If we do not understand it we can't have it apart of our group or society. It is something that I am on the watch for all the time. The reason for this is, I used to be the one picked on or was different in a crowd. I understand how it feels to be the butt of a cruel conversation. I do not mean out right calling someone names or picking on them. What I am talking about is disrespecting them behind their backs or in a way that it hurts them. I realized this from my high school reunion. I was the picked on kid and always wanted to be part of the cool people, or at least who I thought were cool. Then the reunion came and we were all there. I was the most famous person there, doing things in the film industry and trying to make it big. However I was nothing more than the rest, only I had the press. So now when I was at the reunion and I was having a few drinks and shooting the shit. When the most popular girls and there were four I think, came up to me and said that someone wanted to meet me, and I had to guess who it was. I thought to myself, HOLLY SHIT, THEY ARE TALKING TO ME, I felt good. So they brought this girl and presented her to me, she was very good looking, my heart went WOW! Now the girls seeing my expression on my face started to pick and make fun of this beautiful girl. And me wanting to be a part of their group fell into their fun. I asked who it was, they would not let her speak, and they told me who this gorgeous girl was. It was a girl who had a crush on me in school and she was too fat for a fat person. But she had turned her life around and she was great looking. However I did not see that, what I saw were four girls who once were popular and hated this girl for being so beautiful. So they told me her name, and I fell into their cruel humor, and I watch this pretty lady run away crying, because she had feelings for me and I know she did the weight loss for me. I trashed her because I was a low life person at the time. Those popular girls love everything I did, and that day I hurt someone with words and it hurt back. All because I wanted to be one of the cool people, but I found out the cool people were cruel people.

    That is the reason that I will not intentionally cut someone down to gain peer pressure ground. If you are sitting with your friends and someone who is different comes up, I hate it when the group dogs him or her out just because they can. Now mind you I am not against a good ribbing, or roasting a person. But when you say something not so nice just because you cannot think of anything to say. That is not right, it hurts the other person, and it makes you look like a jerk. There is this guy who sits next to me, and he is a nice enough person, but he is irritating, in his mannerisms. You have to understand the person, to understand why they are the way they are. I try to be a friend and co-worker to him, but some of the stuff he does bugs me, one is that every time you talk to him, he starts to play with his groin. I mean come on now, my balls itch once in awhile but all day long, or every time you talk with the person, his hand grabs his nuts. He also has this very high-pitched laugh, and he makes sure that everyone within a square block knows he is laughing. He is starved to be a part of the group, and when someone shows him a little bit of attention, he turns into the wired little dog. Sometimes I almost thought he was going to pee himself. I do not mind talking to him or helping him out. However I do tell him to calm down now and then. The group is starting to talk about him behind his back, and sometimes what they say I think is funny. But this is the start of an outright person bashing. I have seen it before, and I try not to get involved. I try not to judge these people, there is nothing I can do to change their minds, but they do listen to me and take heed as to what I say and do. I am currently trying to steer the bashing to a good part. To make him a part of the team, instead of an outsider, it is hard enough to keep my own life in check, and then have to be responsible for others. I try not to humiliate people in front of others. I make jokes and yes they are pretty bad, however if they are aimed at someone, it will not hurt them. They are starting to call this guy squeaky, because of his high pitched laugh, I can tell he does not care for the name, and I do not call him that. However he will take the name on to be a part of the group. A note to myself, I will stop this, it will bring nothing but sadness for him. There is no need for this, the work environment we work in and so does he, is high enough without adding some childish game to it.

Now on the other side of me in the same row, sits a man starting out in the corporate world. I can tell he will go far, and he will do well. However he has a low threshold for patience. He is very high strung, and gets pissed at the drop of the hat. Now his anger is directed toward computers or desks or any inanimate object. Which is good, because I and anyone else do not need to have a guy going postal. He puts himself under a lot of pressure and I know it stems from his father. Hell it sounds like I am some kind of backyard Shrink or something. I guess everyone is some kind of shrink in their own rights. Everyone has their opinion, even this computer that I am writing this book on has it's own opinion. Every time I write the word their it asks me if I want to substitute (his or her) in place of their. Give me a break! We are all so caught up in politically correct and what is right and wrong with our lives that we forget that TELL'EM ANYTHING is the very thing we are doing. We really don't care about the thing we scream about, we just want to hear that it is all right. Well I hate to be the one to tell you. IT AIN'T ALL RIGHT, it will never be all right and there isn't a thing you can do about it. SO WHY WORRY YOURSELF ABOUT IT. I watch good people go down the tubes because they think that a good moral position in life will change the world. Well it won't, you have to be tough and out going, and willing to risk it all to make changes. If you are that kind of person you will make sacrifices to achieve the things you care about the most. I will tell you now, if you are not the kind of person that is willing to lay it all on the line, you will forever be a person who sits in a chair with a beer in the hand yelling at some politician on TV. These are the very same people that think their vote doesn't count. So they do not vote either. Please if you think yourself moral and well mannered that is great please do not change. However do not bark and yell at me because things do not go your way. That is one of the reasons that I began this book. One, I thought the stories that I ran across in my trek of corporations and the life they create for people is funny. Second, I hope some of the insight that I am sharing will make others think about what is going on around them. And third I have already been told in a suggested manner, that I should not write this book. Can you believe that? I was told that I should not write the truth about what happens behind the walls of corporate America. I am not giving out great secrets, I do not know about any money laundering or IRS evasion. None of that, I am telling stories that I experienced or others I know experienced. These stories and people give the inside knowledge of what corporations think and how they look at the working person. Well maybe that is why they do not want me to write this book. They have lived and prospered off the sufferings of the workers and been doing very well at it. If you really want to know the truth, I too am living off these people. Just by writing this book telling the tales of the worker, is that not living off the workers? However maybe I can change things for the worker in the corporate office. Maybe I can open an eye or two, or just make you stop and think a moment about what is really happening at the work place.

In the chapter READING THE SIGNS, I was talking about watching what is happening around you and who is affected. Well in the last few days, our manager came down hard on us. Our numbers were low and sales were shitty, even after they just hung this huge sign in the lobby telling us how great we all were. But something was in the air. You could feel it. We had special meetings to increase the numbers and to be yelled at. They the managers in a round about way said that some of us were on the block to be canned. Me for one am always ready to be canned. If you are not ready it will be a surprise and then you are up shit creek without a paddle. So as we sat there being chewed out for our numbers, the shit was in the wind. Everyone was on edge, no one knew who was going to get the ax. The betting tables were up, figuratively anyway. Everyone on my team was looking at each other trying to figure out who was meal of the week. Then it happened, we knew it was going to happen and it did. You can tell by the air in the building a lot of people died. It was mostly managers, which came to a shock for many especially the mangers. They did the tornado thing through the marketing department also. Our manager was not fired but he turned from black to white and then back to black again. He thought he was on the way out. However if you know anything about corporate law, you knew he was not on the block. He has too much to offer the company at this time. When he becomes dead wood, as we all will some day, then they will ax him too. And I am sure they will ax me too. Which is why I am glad you are reading this book, I am hoping that it will help you in corporate life, however, I do not want to TELL'EM ANYTHING, I want to make money off this puppy so I do not have to work at companies like that. I love to write and doing what one loves is what is most important.

I have discovered in my trials and tribulations of corporate life and law, you connect to some people and not so well to others. The trick is to juggle the ones that you do not connect to feel that they are still a part of what is happening. People hate to be alienated and made to think they are outcasts. So don't make them outcasts, make them part of your personal team. I have a friend who works in a different department. He busts his ass and makes less than I do. However the stress in my department is higher. Well he has to play under a different set of rules, and for his rules to work their orders that he cannot handle. So I made an arrangement so that he will kick the orders up to me and I will fill the order and take care of the client and cut him in on the profits. It works well for him, it helps me out on the slow times, I pay him the money and everyone is happy. Now comes the bad part, if the company got wind of this, then he would get fired and maybe so would I.

There are so many things that go on within the corporate walls, and it is not mine nor is it your job to keep track of them all. All you can do is keep your area covered and make sure the fall out of other areas does not contaminate you.

Now you are probably wondering about the last statement. Well that is normal for a person whose eyes are just opening to what is going on around them. I was having a conversation with my manager and he was doing an evaluation on me. All companies do this every few weeks or so. It is a way to keep track if their employees are doing their jobs or not. Now it is good for a corporation to keep track. You have to know if what is needed within the work area is being done or not. I must say now that these evaluations are information that is used against the employees later on when they have to fire them. If you think I am crazy, here is a story that happened to me. I was working for a telemarketing company; it was a position I took to get over the hump, cash was short and needed the money for bills. Everyone has been in this situation, now mind you I had other work and this position did not matter to me, it did not mean life or death. I was doing my job dialing numbers; well the computer was dialing the numbers. I was good, hell I am the best damn salesman around. You give me the tools and don't change the rules; I will make you money, however that never happens. The company always changes things; it is the way of corporate life. Get used to it or it will be the death of a salesman. Change is the number one rule. Whether the change is for the good or bad it will happen.

So there I am calling on these people, and I was raising money for movies. The company was leaning toward the shyster side. I would profile the clients and pass them over to the closers. Anyway there was this manager who thought; just because she had the title of manager she could rule with an iron fist and no one would question her actions. Surprise! here comes me, and I do not bow down to bullshit. If it was something that was a serious matter I would do what is asked. But this one day I was doing the calls and they were listening in on the monitoring station, and I was if memory services, I was not following the script that she had made up. Which was a stupid script, she couldn't write either. She comes flying over to my little cubical and demands that I sign this write up that she did, she was disciplining me for not following a telemarketing script word for word. I explained that if I followed the script word for word, I would never use my name, I would be saying, HELLO THIS IS NAME CAN I SPEAK TO, well she did not like that at all. Go figure huh. So she wrote me up, and then had the audacity to tell me that I had to sign it. I asked why? She said; because I told you so. I told her that I would not sign it and that is that. It was an unjust document and if I signed it that would mean that I was guilty of doing something that was wrong. And I was not wrong I might have been arrogant and sarcastic, but I was right.

She was pissed and of course I did this so everyone in the room knew what was happening. She made sure everyone in the room knew I was getting written up, so why should I not do the same to her. Everyone hated her anyway. Well the higher ups pulled me in, and asked me why. I told them that since they would listen and back their manager, which they should. It keeps the chain of command running smooth. You cannot undermine your chain other wise the lower end of the food chain would not listen to the managers. I told them just what I thought. And they let me go. What a loss, but I did learn a few things that day. I learned that to confront someone in that way and make them feel inferior is not the way to go, even though it made me feel great. But I lost in the end, however I found out that two weeks later they fired her, because she was a real bitch to the employees. There are many ways to accomplish things in the work area without sticking your neck out. Everyone you work with will want you to do it, they will coach you on what to do, and they will show you who to talk to and what to say. But they will not do it themselves, they know what the outcome would be and you are the sucker that took it to the gates. What I am saying is if you are a leader and want to climb the ladder, you cannot be a sheep. Let's face it most employees are sheep, they do not want to climb the ladder, they want to complain and do nothing. However if you want to climb they will grab your coat tails and hang on. They do not want to do the work themselves but they do want the rewards when handed out.

This brings us to the person you work with that is a good person but you cannot stand to talk to on personal a basis. He is a musician and does his thing at night, which I must say is the way to go. Make sure you do your own thing, and stake your claim in life. I will never cut him down for that, first it is a tough life to play music and practice and do gigs. He is also the type of person that will find ways to cut you down in a conversation just to make himself look good. You must put a stop to this right away. If you let it go on it will get worse, so one day in the midst of a lunch, we were all sitting together and he said something that was a cut down, he said it was a joke, I said no it was not and I would not have it anymore. He asked me why I was getting upset? I told him and everyone around that I am not against a joke or to even have one directed at me, however to be cut down just so you can get your rocks off is not acceptable to me and I will not be part of it. I told him he was crude in is way of doing things. I told him that if he thought of me in that manner why is he even talking to me? In short I told him to fuck off.

Nobody needs that kind of negativity laid on their shoulders. Do not let anyone put you down. If you stand up for yourself then everyone else will stand up for you also. Everyone is different and everyone sees the world through different eyes. If you do not care to look at the world through those eyes, that is fine but do not cut someone down because he or she sees it differently.

When you are working with someone or many people you will always have personalities that collide with each other. This is normal, it is how you deal with or handle the collisions that matter. Some people can handle them better than others. If you cannot deal with someone, let it be known. Do not let it fester until it is out of control. You can still work with the person but 'only' work with them. I think the biggest clash between workers is when two people get together and both are egotistical, and ambitious. Both people will fight for position and both will not back down. One of two things will happen; one will be that both will end up being separated. Two: they will find a happy medium, that is they will split up the office into sides or teams. These teams will have the people that they can recruit to their side or cause.

It is sad that many situations like this arise. Here is one that I knew the answer to, but needed to find out for myself. My manager is a good one but as I have said before he is naïve when it comes to the world of the corporation life style. However he just might want to be that kind of person, in which he has to wade through all the shit that is dug up. For the past few weeks he has been trying to get his computer fixed at home. He lives the false ideals that the company sets up. He is a survivor and he will do what ever is needed of him from who ever is in charge at the time. He is always touting about responsibility to the company and the way it treats and handles employees. He does not want to be the bad guy. He is also the type of person that when a problem arises he is the first to point out what you did wrong or what you should have done. He says he is there to help but in reality he is one of the best TELL'EM ANYTHING type people around. He will not stick his neck out for anyone or think for himself unless he gets approval from his higher ups. Anyway he wanted me to fix his system. I am a busy man and I do many other things in life that to me are way more important than what he thinks I should be concerned with. So time and time again he asked and asked me to come and look at the system. Now I charge 65 to 75 dollars to fix computers systems for clients. He wanted me to do this for free. Well the day that I decided to do it was when he gave me an electronic Rolodex. It was not working at the time and I fiddled with it and got it working, so I set up a time to do the system for him. I must say at this time that he is not a punctual person he loves to play the (I am important person so I will make people wait). To me he is nothing and should not make me wait. I know that sounds harsh, but when I arrived at the location which is a few blocks from his other home, he was late almost thirty minutes. He knew the time and had three days to get there. This is unacceptable behavior from someone who wants respect. He was using me to get something he needed. I can tell that he wanted to get to know me and do it on safe ground. I came to this conclusion because the computer that was in need of repair is sitting in a location that no person in his or her right mind would ever use it, it was on a bookshelf and sat about four and a half feet off the floor with no chair or desk or anyway to read the screen unless you stood up. So I was checking it out and he continued to ask if I wanted to play golf or go and hit some balls. I will give him this, the system is broke and I did bring it home to work on it in a better location. So I was doing some probing of my own, and found out the president and author of the letter, (few pages back) is a person he wants to get in bed with. I knew then and there where I stood and why I was there and what was needed from me. He did all the stuff companies do to get you to lower your guard. Hell I do all this stuff when I take a client out to dinner or try to cut a deal. However both client and I know that is the way things are done. My manager was using me to practice his technique at negotiating and information collecting. He also knew that I was probing for information. He used to be a good guy, I guess he still is but he will learn the hard way and there is nothing I can do. He will find out that after all the bullshit he is putting up with; he will have to move to another company to gain from what he has learned. He was sort of shocked to find out that I made so little. He was probing me to find out if I wanted to be a manager or where my thoughts were when it comes to the company. I should not worry about it too much, however it does give me good stories to write about. I also dropped a hint to him about this book. I told a little about what the book is about, and told him I was doing stories on corporate laws and life styles. Now my manager is a person that wants to climb the ladder and he will use others to get there. This is just what I want him to do. He has a habit that is not good when it comes to companies and their middle management, he runs off at the mouth trying to impress. For this reason he gets his nuts in a twist now and then.

So if he were fishing for information on me and what I thought and where I stood, I would plant this in him because I know he will tell the higher ups in the company. This in turn will make the higher ups think twice about how they deal with me.

It shows the management that I am somebody that knows the stakes and knows how the game is played. I used their spy or stool pigeon to send information back to them. He is so transparent and this is one of his down falls. I know for a fact this man should not play poker; he would loose his ass, me I am still working on the cold face routine. Now on a better note of the day, this little adventure took me to the ocean area of town, which I do love so much, and we did the driving range thing. I must tell you I am one not to brag unless I feel like it. He was telling me how he went golfing with the other managers and how he was doing well. Well out on the range he was not doing well, but he is learning, and I tell you if there is one thing to be learned about golf and business, is it is a perfect place to make deals and hash out problems. However you must learn to play the game. Golf this time and not the laws of corporations, even though both go together.

What is funny about all this is I use to be just like him, I was a bad golfer and I tried to learn and use the laws of business. I fell on my face a lot, but I learned and I am still learning. And so shall he.

Some quick rules when playing golf with a prospect or client. You should never play fast; you do not know how the other person plays. You should learn to pace yourself with your client; it is like a con artist or a car salesman. They make sure they are progressing at the same pace as their target. They walk the same way the client is walking and take them by the arm almost leading them. When making conversation with the person, you never come out and say what is on your mind. You TELL'EM ANYTHING, it is small talk, find out what they like or need. I am telling you by the time you finish 18 holes of golf you know a lot about the other person. Oh I forgot never get a cart, unless it is lunch golf. Most of the conversations take place walking to get the ball. A golf cart does not give the time needed to make the right impression.

I must say at this time, I have just gotten home from another day on the job. It has become apparent that the cubical world of offices is the new sweatshops of the future. Unlike the sweatshops of old where physical hardship was the cause of pain. The new world sweatshops are mental pain. It is harder to see and harder to prove. They are fast becoming places where the worker has no control of his or her life. It is demeaning work and many corporations use the employees as throw a ways. They know that there will be a new person to fill the spot. Today was a new twist on the ideals of corporate manipulation. The company knew that they were in big trouble because of a serious morale killer. They lied to the employees and gave them a sense of hope. The next day they fired over sixty people. It sent fear running rampant through the company. No one knew if they were next on the chopping block or not. I talk of this problem in another chapter. What I wanted to bring to light today was what they did to rectify the problem. They decided to replace all the monitors on our floor with brand new seventeen-inch color monitors.

Is this a good idea or a bad one? Sometimes it is hard to see what waits in the dark recesses of the corporate mind. Ok so we have monitors, let us really take a look at why a company who is crying poverty goes and spends ten thousand dollars on equipment that is or is not needed. One of the reasons that I heard was, with bigger monitors the employees can look at more windows and production will increase. I had to laugh at this one. First if you cannot find the product on a small monitor, how in the hell are you going to find it on a big one? Or if the product is not in stock, how is a bigger monitor going to make it appear in the warehouse?

SIGNS OF THE TIMES

This is one of my favorite topics when it comes to corporate life. You can tell there is change in the air just by watch the signs within the corporate structure. There are sometimes huge signs and sometimes small signs. But all tell what is blowing in the wind, if you know how to read them.

It takes time to learn the signs, where to find them and how to read them. Everyone within the corporate structure thinks that by reading the trades you know what your company is going to do. This is one of the biggest misconceptions around. The public only knows what is going on with the corporation, after it has been settled as to what to share with the public. Now that I have you totally confused, let me try and explain the thinking here.

In a corporate structure, no one person says we are going to do this or that. There are surveys, and market analysis that tell people what is happening. There are demographics to be studied. Business plans to go over, and even consultants that give advice on which road to travel in the business world. What it comes down to is, no corporation is going to make serious changes or business decisions with out the research. Information is the most important piece of corporate survival, it will tell you when to do something. It will tell you if the idea has a chance of producing profit or causing your competition to fold. It will tell you if your stockholders are nervous or if they are daring. It will tell you if you are doing a good job or a bad one. It will tell you when to quit or when to run in some cases. It will tell you if you are history in the company or if you are moving up the ladder.

But how do you read the signs? This is a tough one, reading signs is one that originates in the gut. It is a feeling or a vibe or something else within you. No it is not a spiritual or religious experience. You have to learn to trust your own feelings and how they work. People say that when a couple stay married long enough they take on the traits of their significant other. This is not true, what is true, is they know the other person so well that they being to anticipate them and their needs. This comes from time served. It is the same in a company. When you have been with a corporation long enough you learn the signs of how the company operates. How many times have you heard a co-worker tell you "SOMETHING IS UP" and you ask them why did they say that? In turn they say Mr. Or Mrs. So and So is not them self today. How does this person know this? What is it that makes them think this way? It is time in service. They know what the higher ups do and how they act. They know if they are serious or just blowing smoke. You learn to read the signs in the office. How about the statement "THE TENSION IN HERE IS SO THICK YOU CAN CUT IT WITH A KNIFE", this too is reading the signs. Signs are emotions that others portray to others. It is either done consciously or unconsciously, however it is done, it is readable. Everyone in the company knows the signs after they have been there awhile. Take payday, it is always a happy one. Everyone knows the cash is there and they will be off for the weekend to spend it. Have you ever been in a company that had a payroll problem and you could not get your check for a few hours? It starts to look like an angry mob. You read the signs and you either get out of the way or you join in. All within hours of each other, some call it mood swings, others just call it what it is, pissed off employees.

Take these shootings in the work place. Going postal is a funny joke around a stressed out office. But how funny is it when a company allows such stress to build to the point of someone walking in with a gun and shooting all the employees, and mostly directed at the dog bitch managers. How can anything get that out of hand? It is the ultimate of TELL'EM ANYTHING, the corporate people do not want to hear about or deal with any problems. So the executives use a rule that comes from history. If the messenger brings bad news, then they kill the messenger. So what happens is the messenger knows the truth about what is going on, and he wants to keep his job and not get fired. So what does he do? He TELLS THE EXECUTIVE JUST WHAT HE OR SHE WANTS TO HEAR. So nothing gets done to help relieve the stress and it begins to build. It never happens over night, stress in the work place is like a thief in the night; it will rob you of your castle, and your family, and then your money. Then you carry this thief back to the place it was born. It will find things to steal, friends, co-workers, clients and more. So this employee who everyone likes, sits there wondering why this has happened. Everyone is TELLING HIM WHAT HE WANTS TO HEAR; no one is worried about his problems. Everyone knows that they are just a few steps behind him. They hate him for showing what they are headed for, so this great employee sees nothing else, no way out. He must kill this thing of stress that has taken everything he lived for. So his mind is made up, if he is going to die and his life is worth nothing to a company who he has given his soul to, then he or she will make sure the company feels his or her pain. One of the saddest things is that most of these ultimate acts of stress can be cured or fixed before reaching that stage of reaction. However no one, not even the co-workers or friends will help. The solution in their minds is a drink might calm him or her down. No this is wrong; they need someone to talk to and to understand what is happening. They do not want to be pitied, you pity these people and you will be first on their shopping list when they come calling. You need to be the friend they think you are. Or the friend you say you are. What is interesting in reading signs is somebody that is headed down the road of destruction gives warning signs all the time. Somebody always knows that they have gone off the deep end. However the signs are not dramatic they are small and they add up. It is like that little itch you can't scratch. You know something is there but just can't put your finger on it. No one wants to pry to far into someone else's problems; hell we all have enough problems without taking on another person's troubles. Take drinking and driving, how many times have you really taken a friends keys from him or her, just so they do not drive under the influence. You always come up with some reason that makes you feel better about letting your friend drive drunk. I did and now he is dead. But I knew he was going to end up dead sometime, so I stopped riding with him also. It is good for me, but I did nothing to help his pain. He was calling out and I refused to see the signs. Here is a little thought that just came to me. The last sentence I was going to say was I DID NOT SEE THE SIGNS, but it really was I REFUSED TO SEE THE SIGNS, I did not want to get involved. Now he is dead and I know it is not my fault. I did not have anything to do with it; I was miles away and in another city when he died. But I also did not try to help him with his problems either. I pushed him away just like everyone else around him. That is when I started to understand that signs and signals others give off could be very helpful. I study body language and read books on the subject. It is one of the most fascinating subjects I have ever learned. There are drawbacks though, when you study people and they way they act, you take an interest in them. This is good, however most people can read you, and when they read my body language they do not know how to interpret it. They become uncomfortable, and do not know how to act. This is all done without words mind you. It is funny because I was uncomfortable because they were uncomfortable, the men thought I was gay and wanted sex with them. The women also thought I wanted sex with them. Maybe Freud was right; maybe all emotions are sexually driven in some form.

Being able to read people makes me a very good sales person or negotiator. However, it also makes me hard to deal with on a long-term basis. I have been able to recognize this in myself and I cannot turn it on and off. I use it to deal with clients and people that are under stress. I can see things in the office workers that they know is there but do not know what it is. I think everyone should learn a little about body language and the way people act. Let's face it, I love to write stories and movie scripts, which makes me a people watcher. How many times have you ever gone to the mall and just watched as people passed by? I would suggest you do it sometime and see the wide variety of people.

The study of people is something that actors and negotiators do. It is something only half of the sales people learn. However sales people inadvertently learn to read their clients. They know when and if they are going to buy. They know when it is the right time to put the pressure on and close the sale. These are good tools of the trade and should be used.

If you learn to read the signs you will understand people more and know what they want out of life. You can also learn when they are bullshitting you or really interested in you. This is very good on a date; you can tell if you will be on first base or in the gutter at the beginning of the date. Then you do not have to waste a good evening with someone who does not want to be with you. Now if you are a good salesperson you can sell yourself to the hard sell and still close escrow. My point is when these shootings, mass firings, or some major upheaval happens or occurs within your corporation, don't be shocked! The only ones that should be shocked are the new people. They have not been there long enough to learn the signs.

Ok now that the melodrama is over. Let us get down to reading the signs of corporate life. Mind you now, that nothing is set in stone. But corporate employees follow a set of rules and regulations. These rules or laws are pretty much standard throughout the industry. Running down the list are, all corporate executives must dress a certain way. The proper clothing; suit and tie for men and for the women in business attire. Just a quick reminder; women have two agendas to deal with. First they must present a professional appearance, and second they must keep their femininity. This is a tough position to be in, because if they swing to far in either direction they will not be taken seriously at their job. I know it sucks but if you do not want to here the truth I could TELL YOU WHAT YOU WANT TO HEAR. If that would make you feel better, truth being it is tougher for a woman to compete in the executive world than a man. It is as simple as that; they must work harder and at lesser pay. I hate to be the one to tell the entire equal rights people but there is nothing you can do to change the minds of the power players. All you do is make them do the most natural thing, TELL'EM ANYTHING and they will tell you anything you want to hear. The only way it will change is with time and teaching our children that prejudices, sexist, and religious preference, etc. Just remember every joke you tell and every person you scorn will leave a lasting impression on your child. So if your child grows up hating a particular group of people, he or she learned it from someone. So do not blame the world for ill will.

Well as we move on, I have to interject this little tad bit of thought. Our society will not allow total peace from prejudice. It is one of the factors that keep our country and every other country moving. Am I crazy? Most likely, but consider this, what would it be like if we did not have prejudice in the world? No need for military, no need to keep the police force so high. It would be equal pay across the board. No one would care what part of town you would live in. Everyone would be the same in standing and social grace. The fact be known everyone is prejudice and there is nothing we can do about it, except try and live together. Ok now that I am off my soapbox, and I am sure I pissed off a few more people. I can apologize, but would that not be telling you something you want to hear to make you feel better. What did you think, with all these groups and not just the women's organizations, running around screaming about save this or save that, equal rights, reform. It is driving me crazy; sure they are trying to do good, but what they are doing is making people lie. Example: the automotive industry needs to follow the clean air law in some states. It must help to clean the air, so what the companies do is buy junk cars that pollute the air and crush them. This falls under the clean air act. So they are doing their part. First let me say, if you really wanted to clean the air, then make a law stating you cannot drive a gasoline powered car period. That is the truth now isn't it? But it is unrealistic, for one I love my car, I pass the emissions test and I follow the law to the letter. However at one time I owned a car that did not pass, so what was I to do? I followed the law and did everything I could to make it pass, but it didn't, so the state made me pay more money and now I can pollute the air. So I ask you, what has all this yelling and screaming done? The air is cleaner because the cars are more efficient, and what did the politicians and the auto industries do? THEY TOLD YOU WHAT YOU WANTED TO HEAR, oh do not get me wrong. There are things that need to be brought before the public.

But the public has a short attention span, and the corporation knows this. Example; two, The Exxon Valdez, now here is something that happened a few years back, people screamed and yelled when this happened. I ask you now; do you really think it is cleaned? It just is not news worthy anymore. The public forgot, so you folks go right on yelling and screaming and our politicians will go right on organizing new study groups with our money to study what you are yelling and screaming about. TELL'EM ANYTHING has got to be the new election campaign slogan.

You have to learn the signs. You must be able to read and understand what is happening around you. If you do not then you will be told WHAT YOU NEED TO HEAR. I do love this subject, people are naïve by nature, they do not want things complicated, they want what was TOLD TO THEM IN SCHOOL, a spouse, a house, a car, a cat, a dog, etc. THE AMERICAN DREAM, the only thing American is the constitution, and if we lose that we lose everything. However, too many lawyers are chewing at it as I am writing this book. Little by little they take away the very thing that made this country. As they chew they TELL US IT IS TO PROTECT US, from whom? Who are they protecting and from whom is this protection against? I have yet seen a communistic invasion in my back yard. So if I am here and you my friend are here, and our country is here, and no one else, who is it.

Forget that, that is too big of a subject to deal with in this book. And don't tell me I am copping out. Because I am, I want to stay on the subject of reading the signs. It is funny many of my co-workers make sport of me because of the way I think and do things. It is, as you can tell, not run of the mill thinking. I like reading between the lines, I love conspiracy theories they make you think. I am not an extremist, however you take a lot to the extremes. I have been burned a few times because I was not reading between the lines. The TELL'EM ANYTHING is everywhere, in everyday life. Advertising is a big one, are they selling you a car or the women in the ad? You cannot drink until you are twenty-one, but you can die for your country at eighteen.

When it comes to reading the unwritten rules of corporations you must understand corporate law. I do not mean the by-laws and governmental laws. The laws are ones that are not set in stone, the ones for everyday operation. Example: Dress code, this one is a good one. It does play a very important part in corporate life. The saying DRESS FOR SUCCESS is true. If you look like a winner then you are a winner. It is a perceived rule, if you look like a slob and want a million dollar deal; the odds are against you obtaining the million-dollar deal. This does not mean you cannot handle a million dollar deal, what it means and the other person read the signs as YOU DO NOT HAVE THE RESPECT ENOUGH TO DRESS FOR THE MEETING. So you lost a deal on perception. The saying is so true; YOU NEVER GET A SECOND CHANCE TO MAKE A FIRST IMPRESSION. Now dressing well for the situation or meeting is the same thing as TELL'EM ANYTHING, it is bullshit. Why is it BS? Because a million dollars was lost on what he did not get. So this means that you have to SHOW'EM ANYTHING too. They do not want to see a slob, so you give them what they want. Weather it is the truth or not. How many times have you seen or been with a wealthy person man or woman, and seen them in casual clothing. Only on the private side of their life, they tell you that this is how they dress. But when it comes to business, they give them what they are looking for.

It is the TIFFANY RULE, you give a gift in a TIFFANY BOX and the perceived value just went up. You give the same gift in a brown sack, you get a totally different perception.

So when in the work place and they have a dress code, it does have a value toward the company. It makes the workers feel more important and part of the corporation and its overall business. This also establishes a foundation for the management of the company. However it also establishes a foundation for the employees as well. Now that a dress code has been decided on, and everyone is following the rules or codes the best they can, you can start to look around and find who are the serious people and who are there for the ride.

Let us look at the tie on the men. Does it loosen after the second hour at work? Does the employee come in not wearing it and put it on after they get there? Does the employee take it off right at quitting time? Is the top button on his shirt button or unbuttoned? Are the cuffs on his shirt also unbuttoned? Mind you now, these same rules apply to the managers and executives as well. Is this person taking the dress code to the edge and trying to see how far they can push it? It is true that in our society clothing is a statement maker. The real trick is what statement is being made and which statement do you want to make? You can tell you co-workers that your tie is choking you. And then you tell your manager that you have been busting your ass all day! TELL'EM ANYTHING does apply here also. It does not matter if this person is working hard or not. Now let us take a look at the higher ups, this is how you can tell if something big is happening. Most executives will wear suit and tie. However if the higher up thinks he or she is better than the employees he or she will walk around not following the rules. Why should he or she? No one will question the fact, and if they do they will change the subject to put you on the defense. Such as why are you worried about my dress, you are the one with low numbers or sales. It is your job you should be worried about. Statements like these are sure signs that, they or the executives do not believe in the rules that they have set for the company. Even the owner of the company will walk around dressed in proper code, if he cares for his company. If he does not then he only cares what he can get out of the company. Anyone that has pride in what they are doing will show it. If you do not have a lot of money you still dress the best you can and try to present yourself in a professional manner in which they want to see. If you do not care, and have a lot of money it still, will show in they way you dress. You will not worry if your shirt is out a little bit or if your tie is not fixed right. It is little things that can be read by anyone looking for the signs. Signs are all over the place, it is sometimes a change in habit or looks or it is just a feeling that you have. The question is why do you have that feeling, something you saw or heard, smelt, touched or sensed told you something was a little bit different. Psychologists use these senses or feelings to see if their patients are making any progress or not. We are creatures and animals of senses, if you use your senses in the right way you can tell a lot about a person. Some people choose to ignore their senses or feelings; they think that they are better than that. They think they can control their lives without the basic instinct in each one of us. But how wrong they are, everyone uses these senses everyday just to survive our world. In the corporate world you can use these senses in the same way. You can read which way the tide is flowing in the corporate river. Once you walk in the door you know if it is going to be a good day or a day you have to watch your back. All this without talking to anyone, sometimes you can feel it in the lobby of the building, with no one around. You just have this sense that something is wrong or right and your body and mind starts to gear it self for the on coming barrage of good or evil. Ok let's say that your VP is a person that always does the same thing. I.E. is clean-shaven and gives a good impression to the workers. Then one day something is not right. He has a five o'clock shadow at nine in the morning. Ok maybe he forgot to shave, but why? Here is a person that has been doing the same routine for months or years. And all of a sudden he forgot something. I have known a lot of executives that have forgotten to shave. However they always have an electric razor in the office desk. They even have extra shirts and ties. They are ready for anything that might happen. If they are at lunch and spill a cup of coffee on themselves, they have an extra shirt to get them through the meeting that is coming up. So my mind starts to ask questions, why is this person doing a change, like growing a beard?

This is not the proper way to grow a beard, do not get me wrong a beard is ok, however you do not grow one when serious business is pending. The first month of growth makes you look like a bum. If you want to make a drastic change like that you always start it on your vacation so the rough part is out of sight of the business professionals. Other wise you send signals to everyone in the place that you are not happy with something and you are looking for a change. The reason why men grow beards is because it is a drastic change of looks and you are hiding yourself from the inevitable whatever that maybe. It could mean that there are serious changes happening in the work force, and the executive that has to do the firing of underlings do not want them to be angry at him so he hides behind a beard. Or it could me that his shit is in the wind and he does not want anyone to remember what he looks like after he is gone. That way he can have a fresh start at another company. If you look for the signs within that company, you will have a better chance at surviving the ax of fear when the executives start yelling at everyone when the quarterly reports come out. Let's face it no matter how good the report is, the executives will always find something that is not right. It starts out like this, I WOULD LIKE TO CONGRATULATE EACH AND EVERYONE OF YOU ON A JOB WELL DONE. WE HAVE PASSED OUR GOAL FOR THIS QUARTER; HOWEVER WE STILL NEED TO WORK ON THIS OR THAT, does this sound familiar? If the company stops the pressure on the employees, even for a day, it will take a month to get everyone moving again. The entire company will take a break, and it is like starting all over again. The company must keep the momentum going. This brings up a saying that I heard; hell my brother told me this one; IT TAKES SIX "THAT A BOYS" TO OFFSET ONE "OH SHIT", I do like that saying. It is so true, think about it, it is hard to get a pat on the back, but if you screw up they are all over you. It is like a pack of wolves waiting on the crippled dear. The wolves will not attack a strong animal, however, if you become weak, your ass is grass. How do you keep the wolves at bay? You TELL'EM ANYTHING, make sure they hear and see what they want. You toss them some meat and they are happy. There came a day, I knew the company was putting on the pressure of the managers to increase sales. The reason I knew this was I was watching the signs, there was an extra managers meeting and all the mangers were buzzing around trying to look busy instead of huddled in the group BS session they always have. So the managers took out their imaginary clubs and started beating the teams. Of course the strong members did not get a beating, they got a tap, which was a show tap, it was to show the weaker ones that they the managers were not picking on them only.

So they walked around beating everyone, then when they were done with that, they were walking around asking everyone to convict themselves with a poor work performance so they can use it against them later. They came around asking what could you realistically do each month. So all these naïve people gave a number, which was half of the number, the company wanted. This was a bad move, for everyone that said a different number than the one presented to them. When the manager came to me and asked. WHAT DO YOU THINK YOU CAN DO THIS MONTH? I answered fourteen thousand, which was the number they told me I had to reach. The manager looked at me, and said

THIS IS NOT TO BE USED AGAINST YOU; they were trying to prove to the executives that the numbers were too high for the teams to reach. I asked THEN WHY ASK US IF WE CAN REACH A NUMBER, just set it lower. We bantered back and forth over this, and I would not reverse myself. I told him that I would do everything in my power to reach the numbers. He is a good manager but he is naïve, and the company will use the numbers against me. I have been there before. He was in shock, I think he took it personally but that is his problem.

The company will tell you it is for tracking purposes and then use it to beat you up. Very seldom will they look at something good and tell you it is good. They always look for the bad; it is the only thing they know.

I tried to explain to him the reason why, but he would not listen he thought I was being difficult, but all I was doing was covering my ass. It works like this, I am your friend and I am trying to help you out. Then a few months pass and something happens, they reach into their bag of tricks and pull that very thing out and use it against you. This is something that I have learned over years of dealing with the corporate lifestyle and corporate survival. You too will learn this, and yes you will learn it the hard way. Just like a teenager who thinks they know everything and learns the hard way. I was the same way when someone tried to help me out and show me the ropes. I would not listen either, and for my failures of not learning and listening, I was burned because I did not read the signs.

Stress is another sign that can be read. It makes people different, in their actions and the way the deal with problems and situations. When someone is under pressure, it is hard to help him or her out because you see the problem in a different light. The trick is to show them the problem in a different way without setting them off. This is what a friend is for, however when someone is under the stress factor they tend to bark at everyone around them. Even if your intentions are meant well, they cannot see that you want to help them. So most people will stick their head in the proverbial hole in the ground and wait until it blows over or blows up. The thing is, you can read the signs of this person and know that they are having a hard time with the project at hand. What we have not been taught is, how to handle situations like this. Most companies and people for that matter do not want to deal with it. The reason why they do not want to deal with it is because they do not know how to deal with. If they knew what to do, they would jump in and help out. But our society has taught us that if we get involved with something and it goes wrong, you become the scapegoat, and your life is trashed. It is the same thing when it comes to crime in the streets. The police mean well and use the TELL'EM ANYTHING just so they can catch the people who did the crime. They tell you WE WILL PROTECT YOU, but everyone knows they cannot. So the witnesses just say they did not see anything. Which makes the police's job harder and everything starts to escalate. Frustration increases and the pressure is turned up, until someone does something that breaks the camels back, and that person is the focal point of the stress that has been building up. Then what happens, we blame the police for being bad boys, and sue the city for all the money we can get. But we never look at the real cause of the problem or why it happened. And the pressure starts to build again, and it will be released again. It is a never-ending cycle, unless we want to end the cycle. As long as we continue to look to someone else to solve our problems, we will always have our problems. I attended a private discussion group with some of the top PR firms in the country. I had never met these people before, however I did know them and who they were. I was doing a presentation for them, which turned into a three-hour discussion about marketing, public relations, and sales and how they all affected each other. We came to a conclusion that failure comes down to two factors and two factors only. The reason that anything fails whether it is business or just poor performance on the job is FEAR or IRRESPONSIBILITY; you can trace all failure to one of these two factors. From the largest corporation to the smallest project these two factors are the foundation as to the downfall, of the project, person or corporation.

    If you are good at reading signs, you can see one or both of these factors in a person. You can tell whether they will be around long or if they are out to make life difficult for you. Reading these two signs can clear many hurdles from your path.

Just by recognizing that these are hurdles to overcome or bypass makes your life easier and more efficient.

Be careful even the best of sign readers can be caught off guard. Man I am here to tell you, the company I work for just pulled the biggest snow job I have ever seen. I do have to admit that if it was thought out or planned it was brilliant. However if it was not planned it was a shitty thing to do!

It was the middle of the week and everyone in the place is feeling like long tailed cats in a room full of rocking chairs. You couldn't even fart without someone jumping and screaming. Now that is pressure that is not needed in any work environment. And we knew that the big wigs were sitting in their chairs (rocking chairs) just watching which cubical exploded first. The clock ticked as the hands of time crawled to a stop, or it seemed that way. That was one of the longest weeks I have ever had. You would do anything just to get through it. What is funny is most of the workers did less work and more worrying about their jobs. So in reality the stress or pressure they applied was the turn off knob and it drove the work process to a halt.

They needed something to change the tide of pending doom on the sales floor. So the plan was set, the idea was to have a field trip to one of our manufacturers factories! WOW! Now does that bring back high school! This was the best idea that could come out of BA'S, BS'S, PHD'S and you name it. The brilliant people running our organization went as far as supplying box lunches. Not only did this insult everyone on the sale force, but spending five hours of sales time walking around an automated factory was a complete waste of time. And how did the BULLSHIT fly! Every middle management person could not say enough about how good it was, and the experience plus the knowledge that was gained from this trip. IT WAS THE WORST TRIP I HAVE EVER BEEN ON! I wanted to die, everyone I was with wanted to die, they made us dress up and look pretty for the factory workers. Who, by looking in their eyes, could give two shits about us being there either! It was animals on parade day at the factory.

However the head honchos loved it, they stood next to each other, parading the troops (as they called us) in front of the other troops. The factory was boring! They showed us the lobby and then the store room then the factory floor, which we could not go in, and the research and development room, which we could not go in, the gym and the break room. Oh yea I forgot they took us into the shipping area too. WOW now this was great, then our guide who you knew was volunteered for the position, was forced to ask us if there were any questions. Our group wanted to help and make the man feel good, but what question could be asked without humiliating yourself! No one asked anything, so they marched us into the conference room and gave a speech in front of a banner welcoming us to the factory. Just a note, after the tour almost a third of the sales people said they would never sell their product unless the client asked for it directly. This trip was a very bad idea. It totally trashed morale to the point no one wanted anything to do with the company or its ideals. The next day stats showed more than a fifty percent drop in productivity on following day.

Well it was bad enough to be stuck on a bus, for an hour road trip to the factory and then getting stuck in LA traffic for two and a half hours on the way back. Now comes the coup de grace! After this amazing ordeal that the sales force had to survive, there were members of the sales team who did not survive the ordeal. As soon as we got back home to our own nest, the managers walked up to them and fired them! This was way out of line in my book. First to send these people on that trip and then fire them as they got off the bus, which sucks in anybodies book! That means that they knew they were going to let these people go, and did nothing. Let's take a look at just what they did to the entire sales floor. They fired more than a third not more than a week or so ago, then continued with the firings in other departments the following days. People were walking up and their badges were not working, and if they did not work they were out the door. They sent us on a trip which not only was the worse thing in history but lost sales and clients, because we were not there to service them. The month of August was the morale buster of all times. It started the rats jumping ship and back stabbings between the staff and employees. It was the TITANIC all over again. Since the company building sat on a block, it was without a doubt a blockbuster.

All the while the middle management was telling the TELL'EM ANYTHING tale of how good things are and what the future holds. However it was in the tone of "YES I WILL SAY THIS TO KEEP MY JOB" they have turned serious sales consultants into TELEMARKETERS!

TIME OFF

Everyone has time off from time to time. Whether it comes in the form of vacation or sick leave or just playing hooky. It is important to take some time to regroup your thoughts. You know when you need to get away and have a little time to yourself. Everyone does, however if you are the type who doesn't think they can afford time off. You are the one that's in real need of time off.

Many people think that time off is time to party. This is true to a point, what time off should be is time to mentally regroup your thoughts and attitude. Now you might ask isn't that what camping is or going to the beach? Yes it is, however how many people really get a chance to go to the beach or hike in the mountains, of even visit a park? Not many, and the reason is they are too worried about other things.

I look at time off as a way to increase my chances to get out of the place that I cannot stand to work. Time off is the perfect time to find other means of income and grow it from your home. Home-based businesses are great for this. I know what a lot of you will say. I don't have time to start a home-based business. Or it is too much work or I do not have enough money. Well all that is fine, but don't come to me and say I hate my job or this place stinks. I will in turn tell you I DON'T WANT TO HEAR IT. The reason is I am writing this book on my time off. I make the time to write, and at this moment in time I hope it sells and that way I can always have time to myself while you are complaining that you have no time.

The only reason that you have no time is because you do not want to be successful. It has been said many times by different people, if you want to get something done give it to a busy person. What I am saying is that the weekends are yours and the nighttime is yours. What you choose to do with it is also yours. Let me check something, it is 1:36 in the morning and I am trying to help you make the money everyone wants. All I can do, and all anyone can do is show you what can be done. I cannot do it for you nor can anyone else. You must do it for yourself and family.

You can still work your job and make the kind of living you want. But the company you work for does not own you unless you let them own you. We live in a time were company promises and ideas are not strong enough to bet your future on.

Let us use what the company does all the time. Here is the formula, if you make ten sales today, and you multiply that by five, you have made fifty sales in the week. That is good to the company. Now if you make one sale, selling something from your home, a day. You made five sales in the week. The difference is those five sales, the profit is all yours, so if you figure the sale of one product is twenty buck, let's make it easy. And the profit of the product is five dollars, and the company pays you five percent on the profit you have just made twenty-five cents on the product. So you by the end of the week you have made twelve dollars and fifty cents. Now let's take the five sales at night or at home. The product cost the same twenty dollars, your profit is five dollars and you sold five you have made twenty-five dollars for the week.

You have done this on your time off. You double your income and lessened your work. Why work for someone who is getting profits off of you? It is ok to make someone money if they compensate you in some way. Companies use things like insurance as a ploy to keep you working for them and they will tell you things like. IF YOU WORK FOR YOURSELF YOU HAVE NO SECURITY. Well first prove to me that I have security here! I'm not saying go quit your job and start a home based business, what I am saying is that use your time off so you do not have to worry about retirement, or that extra dollar. You can do anything you want, it is up to you. Shit, when I turn eighty I am going to be driving a sports car and living on the beach, with all my kids waiting for me to kick off so they can have the sports car and the beach house.

There are so many things that can be accomplished with little to no effort, and it can bring in a nice second income or turn into a windfall of cash. You just have to stop being lazy and do it. Which is the very reason why many people do not make ends meet or complain that they are not making enough money to live on. They know what is out there but they do not have the faith in themselves to do it. All it takes is you doing it a few hours a night or on weekends. Then go to the beach and the mountains; play with the kids or the spouse.

I know many of you are saying that your time is too precious; you want to spend it with the family or friends. Ok that is fair enough, turn the TV off and spend time with them. Think about this one for a moment, a TV producer makes money, producing shows. Do you realize the only time he or she watches programs is when they are put on tape and watches them later. Even then they are working, my point is you are watching programs that are done by people who are making money by not watching programs. They are busy doing things at home or in the office. Some of the best ideas for TV shows come to the writers while they are writing for other shows. I'm not saying be a workaholic, just look to the future. However the company you work for relies on this factor. They don't want you doing other things to improve your status in society. They want you just the way you are, that way they know they will get the most out of you before your time comes to leave the company. Ask yourself this, why do so many huge companies, have CEO's or owners over the retirement age? Why don't they retire to the good life? The reason is because they are doing the good life, we just don't see them doing it. They love what they are doing, and rightly so. They built the company with your hard work. I must give them credit too, because they did not sit on their backsides watching TV shows. I must defend myself on the dogging out of TV; I make money off of TV even though I know it is a waste of time. I love to watch as much as the next guy. I have to force myself to get off my butt and finish the projects that I have going on. Or at least work on them. Take this book, I did not write it over night. However I write every night, some nights it is hours and others nights it is minutes. But I make sure that I work on it every day or night. As they say Rome wasn't built in a day. You must do it, just a little bit each day, then one day you will look and say HOLY SHIT I DID IT! Then you will walk into work and say goodbye. Just think, you have an estimated forty-eight hours in a week to do what ever you want. You made the company you're working for a ton of cash in the period of time. Why can't you do the same thing for yourself? I know there are exceptions to everything and yes you can shoot holes in this all day long. But the thing is you can't cover every minute of the day with excuses to why you can't do something. If your car breaks down and you need it for work the next day. And you can't afford a mechanic or have the time to repair it you will do it yourself. You will find the time and work on it long into the night until it is done. You will even call in the next day if you did not finish it. If you put one third of that effort into something that will pull you out of the hole, you will not have to call into work and TELL'EM ANYTHING why you are late. You could have said, ok I will wait until tomorrow and buy another car.

I love time off from work; I get excited about writing or reading someone else's writing. My boss or manager asks me to come over so that I can fix his computer. I tell him it will be no problem. However my time is important, and he has to give me seven days or one week when he wants me to come over to fix his system. He has asked many times and I have told him I must know by this time or that. He never gets around to it; I tell him that it is ok just let me know. I don't waste my time any more on someone who is not ready. If someone tells me that they will be somewhere at such a time I will be there. If they are not there I will leave and it is very hard to get me to come back. Unless it is something I want or need. The point is, waste my time and you won't get me. I have so much time to write and to read the movie scripts and contact the people I need to create my future. I cannot go by the seat of my pants; it is wasteful and expensive, one of the major rules (or is it the unwritten rule) of corporations is the higher up you go the more power you have to make people wait.

One of the best stories that was told to me, I believe it is true but I have no facts as to if it is true. In the heydays of the MARX BROTHERS and they were very popular and commanded the attention of all the studios in Hollywood. It goes like this, one day the MARX BROTHERS had a meeting with a high up executive at WARNER BROTHERS and it was set for a certain time. This high up person thought that he was way too important to be on time for the MARX BROTHERS and had them wait in his office. So after an hour or so he was ready to meet and make a deal with the MARX BROTHERS.

It started good enough, they walked into WARNER BROTHERS executive office and the secretary showed them into mister big shots office. And they waited and waited, what happened next is why the MARX BROTHERS were so famous for, their unpredictability. The big shot opened the door and found all three brothers sitting naked in the middle of his office roasting marshmallows over a fire in the middle of the floor. So the story goes. I have no facts to support this or evidence from which the story was told to me. I must also say that WARNER BROTHERS and MARX BROTHERS are most likely trademarks and belongs to them. The point to the story is the MARX BROTHERS knew the value of time and to waste it was foolish. So they put it to good use, and from that use they never had to wait again. Time is important, don't waste it and don't abuse it.

There is this co-worker that is always complaining that he has no time to finish anything. He stays late and works late, just to catch up. He asks me how I get all my stuff done for the day on time. I look at him and say, I WANT TO GO HOME ON TIME. So I watch him ask the same question to about six people and every person he asks he talks to for about ten minutes. I think you see where I am going with this. If he would do his work instead of asking and talking to everyone, he too can go home on time. Look I mess around as much as the next guy, however I make sure I take care of business. It is important to stay focused on what you want, if you need to get the work done, you must focus on that goal. If you want to complain, then you must focus on that goal. However do not scream and shout if you do not finish in time to go home. These are your choices in life, you make your bed and you must sleep in it. Trust me on this I have slept in some shitty beds and I didn't like it one bit. Also knowing my own personality I know that I will sleep in other shitty beds, but not as many as I used to. Time can be your friend or your enemy, you can use it to make wealth or make someone else wealthy.

Time is one of the most flexible tools at your fingertips. It can be manipulated to your advantage, or it can be manipulated against you. The only thing that cannot be changed about time is it is constant. If you look at it in the right way it will become a strong ally. If you let time control your actions then it will become an enemy that will not stop. We have time built into our lives, even our bodies need time so it can control the functions needed to continue life. Humans are the ones that gave time meaning; nature just does it because it has to. Your heart beats because it has to. You wake up at a certain time because you want to. Your mind subconsciously controls the time your body keeps. And if time is controllable at a subconscious level then it very controllable at a conscious level.

Everything we do is affected by time. Time is pressure that can change a mountain into a valley, or a valley into a mountain. That in itself is power and power is controlling time.

The two things that give you the power needed to change anything are time and consistency. Everything else is built on this concept, wars are won and cities are built. Babies are born within a nine-month span; this is how much time it takes to create a human child. Every company in the world operates on time and what it can achieve within that time frame. Time can be broken down into precise increments, if you need to accomplish something in a certain time, and you know how long it takes to do one part of the project. You can figure out how long it will take you to do that project.

There are many factors needed to complete a project, and those factors all consist of increments of time. Building a building, the contractor knows how fast a man can carry a block to the wall. He also knows how many blocks it takes to build that wall. So with those two pieces of the puzzle he can figure out how long it will take to build the building.

The Grand Canyon took millions of years to produce the effect that it has. You to can build a Grand Canyon, if you were consistent and had the time. My point is that using time will build you the world you are looking for, or it will destroy the world you live in. Both are inevitable and both will come to pass.

So if you understand this from the start you will be able to manipulate time so it works in your favor.

I know that I can type 70 words a minute. I also know that I can do one page in this book a day. If I were going to do, let's say two hundred pages for the book, then it would take me two hundred days to complete the book. Which figures out to be just under seven months. Now if I want to finish it quicker, and still use the same number of pages, I would want to type two pages a day and then I could finish the book in one hundred days or just under four months. Now there are always factors to consider in matters of working with time. However even those factors are time controllable. This is one of the reasons that many companies nowadays use computers. They are more efficient in controlling the time factor. Many companies have learned that if they teach multitasking which is a buzzword within corporate America. They can increase production without increasing labor. You as an employee can finish more tasks at one time. You have twenty-four hours in a day. No one is telling you how to spend those hours. You chose to work at the place you are working. You give that company the permission to tell you how to spend some of those hours that are given to you. What you do with the rest of the hours you still have, you still have the choice in how to utilize them. There are many people out there that will tell you how to spend those remaining hours. Some are good ideas and some are not so good. This is, where free will comes in, it is up to you to chose how to spend those hours. And guess what? IF YOU DO NOT CHOSE TO DO SOMETHING YOU STILL MADE A CHOICE ON HOW TO SPEND THE TIME.

Ouch, I just got back from the job. It is funny that I am working on this chapter entitled TIME OFF, when all we did today was discuss the subject of time. The company continued to tell us THAT IT IS ALL UP TO US AND HOW WE USE OUR OWN TIME. They tell us that if we use it right we will be rich and make lots of money. However after they are done with their speeches they turn around and tell us how they want us to do something. I have never seen a company so indecisive in my life. They want this perfect world and they are living in a dreamland of ideals. The sad thing is they are making it difficult for all the new hires to produce. They will not chastise the old timers with over three years. But the reality is they have hired almost three times as many new people and now they cannot justify the hiring of so many people. Which means some time in the future they will pit the employees against one another in order to save their jobs. It has already started; they have pitted the managers against each other with fear of losing their positions within the company. It is sad, how people are and what they will do to keep a job that does not care if they live or die. My manager asked me point blank if myself and the top salesperson who is a lady, if we would help in handling the team. I said that I would help; however when I attempted to help today, all I got was cold shoulders. So much for the help, he still wants me to fix his computer at his house. I am skeptical about doing it; because it is on unfamiliar ground he will have the advantage. I also know that I am a talkative person, which I must control. He on the other hand is a believer in hopes and promises of corporations. He is new to the game, not to say that I am an old wiz kid. I like the guy, he can be trusted to a point, except when it comes to the company. I just happened to think, he will know or learn the hard way when he reads this book.

www.ingramcontent.com/pod-product-compliance
Lightning Source LLC
Chambersburg PA
CBHW030758180526
45163CB00003B/1084